KEEP A QUIET HEART

Keep a Quiet Heart

Elisabeth Elliot

VB
VINE
BOOKS

Servant Publications
Ann Arbor, Michigan

Vine Books is an imprint of Servant Publications
especially designed to serve evangelical Christians.

Scripture quotations taken from *The Holy Bible: New
International Version* (NIV), © 1973, 1978, 1984 International
Bible Society, Used by permission of Zondervan Bible
Publishers; The New Testament in Modern English by J.B.
Phillips (PHILLIPS), Geofry Bles, Ltd.; *The Holy Bible: Authorized
King James Version*(KJV); *The New English Bible* (NEB); *The
Living Bible* (LB), Revised Standard Version (RSV), Jerusalem
Bible (JB).

Published by Servant Publications
P.O. Box 8617
Ann Arbor, Michigan 48107

Cover photo: Howard M. DeCruyenaere
Cover design: Michael Andaloro

96 97 98 99 10 9 8 7 6 5 4

Printed in the United States of America
ISBN 0-89283-906-6

Library of Congress Cataloging-In-Publication Data

Elliot, Elisabeth.
    Keep a quiet heart / Elisabeth Elliot.
        p.   cm.
    ISBN 0-89283-906-6
    1. Christian life.   I. Title.
BV4501.2.E366   1995
242—dc20   95-6338
                                                    CIP

Contents

Section Two: God's Curriculum

Do Not Rush.
Trust.
And Keep a Quiet Heart.

I think I find most help in trying to look on all the interruptions and hindrances to work that one has planned out for oneself as discipline, trials sent by God to help one against getting selfish over one's work. Then one can feel that perhaps one's true work—one's work for God—consists in doing some trifling haphazard thing that has been thrown into one's day. It is not a waste of time, as one is tempted to think, it is the most important part of the work of the day—the part one can best offer to God. After such a hindrance, do not rush after the planned work; trust that the time to finish it will be given sometime, and keep a quiet heart about it.

Annie Keary, 1825-1879

Introduction

For about a dozen years I have been writing, every other month, what I called a newsletter. It is not a very good title. It's simply a letter meant to cheer and encourage—once in a while perhaps to nettle or amuse—those who want it. There isn't much "news." I include an itinerary of the places where I am to speak, and from time to time I announce the arrival of another grandchild. Sometimes I recommend books.

This book is a compilation of lead articles culled from the newsletter. Mostly they are about learning to know God. Nothing else, I believe, comes close to being as important in life as that. It's what we are here for. We are created to glorify Him as long as we live on this planet, and to enjoy Him for the rest of eternity.

Our task is simply to trust and obey. This is what it means to love and worship Him. Jesus came to show us how that can be done. In the Gospel of John, He is called "the Word."

In the beginning was the Word, and the Word was with God, and the Word was God. He was with God in the beginning.

Through him all things were made; without him nothing was made that has been made. In him was life, and that life was the light of men. The light shines in the darkness, but the darkness has not understood it....

He was in the world, and though the world was made through him, the world did not recognize him. He came to that which was his own, but his own did not receive him. Yet to all who received him, to those who believed in his name, he gave the right to become children of God—children born not of natural descent, nor of human decision or a husband's will, but born of God.

The Word became flesh and made his dwelling among us. We have seen his glory, the glory of the One and Only, who came from the Father, full of grace and truth.

John 1:1-14 NIV

It is reasonable to believe that the One who made the worlds, including this one and us who live in it, is willing to teach us how to live. He "became flesh" in order to *show* us, day by day as He walked the lanes of Galilee and the streets of Jerusalem, how to live in company with God.

The following pages are the musings of a slow learner. It has been well over half a century since I welcomed Christ as my Redeemer and asked Him to be Lord of my life. You will find much repetition of elementary lessons, for I have written as I would to my family and close friends, putting down rather chattily the things by which I was being encouraged, convicted, and strengthened by the Spirit of God.

One rainy afternoon at Wheaton College in 1947 my friend Sarah Spiro and I were at the piano in Williston Hall. I had written down a few lines of a prayer which I hoped was poetry. Sarah studied them for a minute and then set them to music. I haven't a copy of the music, but here are the words:

Lord, give to me a quiet heart
That does not ask to understand,
But confident steps forward in
The darkness guided by Thy hand.

This was my heart's desire then. It is the same today. A willing acceptance of all that God assigns and a glad surrender of all that I am and have constitute the key to receiving the gift of a quiet heart. Whenever I have balked, the quietness goes. It is restored, and life immeasurably simplified, when I have trusted and obeyed. God loves us with an everlasting love. He is unutterably merciful and kind, and sees to it that not a day passes without the opportunity for new applications of the old truth of *becoming* a child of God. This, to me, sums up the meaning of life.

Magnolia, Massachusetts
October, 1994

Section One

Faith for the Unexplained

Thou art the Lord who slept upon the pillow,
Thou art the Lord who soothed the furious sea,
What matter beating wind and tossing billow
If only we are in the boat with Thee!

Hold us in quiet through the age-long minute
While Thou art silent, and the wind is shrill:
Can the boat sink while Thou, dear Lord, art in it?
Can the heart faint that waiteth on Thy will?

Amy Carmichael
Toward Jerusalem

A Quiet Heart

Jesus slept on a pillow in the midst of a raging storm. How could He? The terrified disciples, sure that the next wave would send them straight to the bottom, shook Him awake with rebuke. How could He be so careless of their fate?

He could because He slept in the calm assurance that His Father was in control. His was a quiet heart. We see Him move serenely through all the events of His life—when He was reviled, He did not revile in return. When He knew that He would suffer many things and be killed in Jerusalem, He never deviated from His course. He had set His face like flint. He sat at supper with one who would deny Him and another who would betray Him, yet He was able to eat with them, willing even to wash their feet. Jesus in the unbroken intimacy of His Father's love, kept a quiet heart.

None of us possesses a heart so perfectly at rest, for none lives in such divine unity, but we can learn a little more each day of what Jesus knew—what one writer called the *negligence* of that trust which carries God with it. Who would think of using the word negligence in regard to our Lord Jesus? To be negligent is to omit to do what a reasonable man would do. Would Jesus omit that? Yes, on occasion, when faith pierced beyond reason.

This "negligent" trust—is it careless, inattentive, indolent? No, not in His case. Jesus, because His will was one with His Father's, could be free from care. He had the blessed assurance of knowing that His Father would do the caring, would be attentive to His

Son's need. Was Jesus indolent? No, never lazy, sluggish, or sloth-
ful, but He knew when to take action and when to leave things up
to His Father. He taught us to work and watch but never to worry,
to do gladly whatever we are given to do, and to leave all else with
God.

Purity of heart, said Kierkegaard, is *to will one thing*. The Son
willed only one thing: the will of His Father. That's what He came
to earth to do. Nothing else. One whose aim is as pure as that can
have a completely quiet heart, knowing what the psalmist knew:
"Lord, You have assigned me my portion and my cup, and have
made my lot secure" (Psalm 16:5 NIV). I know of no greater *sim-
plifier* for all of life. Whatever happens is assigned. Does the intellect balk at that? Can we say that there are things which happen to
us which do not belong to our lovingly assigned "portion" (This
belongs to it, that does not")? Are some things, then, out of the
control of the Almighty?

Every assignment is measured and controlled for my eternal
good. As I accept the given portion other options are cancelled.
Decisions become much easier, directions clearer, and hence my
heart becomes inexpressibly quieter.

What do we really want in life? Sometimes I have the chance to
ask this question of high school or college students. I am surprised
at how few have a ready answer. Oh, they could come up with
quite a long list of *things*, but is there *one* thing above all others
that they desire? "One thing have I desired of the Lord," said
David, "this is what I seek: that I may dwell in the house of the
Lord all the days of my life..." (Psalm 27:4 KJV). To the rich young
man who wanted eternal life Jesus said, "One thing you lack. Go,
sell everything" (Mark 10:21 NIV). In the Parable of the Sower,
Jesus tells us that the seed which is choked by thorns has fallen
into a heart full of the worries of this life, the deceitfulness of
riches, and the desire for *other things*. The apostle Paul said, "One
thing I do: forgetting what is behind and straining towards what is
ahead, I press on toward the goal to win the prize for which God
has called me heavenward in Christ Jesus" (Phil 3:13-14 NIV).

A quiet heart is content with what God gives. It is enough. All is grace. One morning my computer simply would not obey me. What a nuisance. I had my work laid out, my timing figured, my mind all set. My work was delayed, my timing thrown off, my thinking interrupted. Then I remembered. It was not for nothing. This was part of the Plan (not mine, His). "Lord, You have assigned me my portion and my cup."

Now if the interruption had been a human being instead of an infuriating mechanism, it would not have been so hard to see it as the most important part of the work of the day. But *all* is under my Father's control: yes, recalcitrant computers, faulty transmissions, drawbridges which happen to be *up* when one is in a hurry. My portion. My cup. My lot is secure. My heart can be at peace. My Father is in charge. How simple!

My assignment entails my willing acceptance of my portion— in matters far beyond comparison with the trivialities just mentioned, such as the death of a precious baby. A mother wrote to me of losing her son when he was just one month old. A widow writes of the long agony of watching her husband die. The number of years given them in marriage seemed too few. We can only know that Eternal Love is wiser than we, and we bow in adoration of that loving wisdom.

Response is what matters. Remember that our forefathers were all guided by the pillar of cloud, all passed through the sea, all ate and drank the same spiritual food and drink, but God was not pleased with most of them. Their response was all wrong. Bitter about the portions allotted they indulged in idolatry, gluttony, and sexual sin. And God killed them by snakes and by a destroying angel.

The same almighty God apportioned their experience. All events serve His will. Some responded in faith. Most did not.

"No temptation has seized you except what is common to man. And God is faithful; he will not let you be tempted beyond what you can bear. But when you are tempted, he will also provide a way out so that you can stand up under it" (1 Corinthians 10:13 NIV).

Think of that promise and keep a quiet heart! Our enemy delights in disquieting us. Our Savior and Helper delights in quieting us. "As a mother comforts her child, so will I comfort you" is His promise (Is 66:13, NIV). The choice is ours. It depends on our willingness to see everything in God, receive all from His hand, accept with gratitude just the portion and the cup He offers. Shall I charge Him with a mistake in His measurements or with misjudging the sphere in which I can best learn to trust Him? Has He misplaced me? Is He ignorant of things or people which, in my view, hinder my doing His will?

God came down and lived in this same world as a man. He showed us how to live in this world, subject to its vicissitudes and necessities, that we might be changed—not into an angel or a storybook princess, not wafted into another world, but changed into saints in *this* world. The secret is *Christ* in *me*, not me in a different set of circumstances.

> He whose heart is kind beyond all measure
> Gives unto each day what He deems best,
> Lovingly its part of pain and pleasure,
> Mingling toil with peace and rest.
>
> **Lina Sandell, Swedish**

∞∞∞

The Angel in the Cell

My brother Dave Howard does a lot of traveling and comes back with wonderful stories. One summer when the six of us Howards with our spouses got together for a reunion, Dave told us this one, heard from the son of the man in the story.

A man whom we'll call Ivan, prisoner in an unnamed country, was taken from his cell, interrogated, tortured, and beaten nearly to a pulp. The one comfort in his life was a blanket. As he staggered back to his cell, ready to collapse into that meager comfort, he saw to his dismay that someone was wrapped up in it—an informer, he supposed. He fell on the filthy floor, crying out, "I can't take any more!" whereupon a voice came from the blanket: "Ivan, what do you mean, you can't take any more?" Thinking the man was trying to get information to be used against him, Ivan didn't explain. He merely repeated what he had said.

"Ivan," came the voice, "Have you forgotten that Jesus is with you?"

Then the figure in the blanket was gone. Ivan, unable to walk a minute before, now leaped to his feet and danced round the cell praising the Lord. In the morning the guard who had starved and beaten him asked who had given him food. No one, said Ivan.

"But why do you look so different?"

"Because my Lord was with me last night."

"Oh, is that so? And where is your Lord now?"

Ivan opened his shirt, pointed to his heart—"Here."

"OK. I'm going to shoot you and your Lord right now," said the guard, pointing a pistol at Ivan's chest.

"Shoot me if you wish. I'll go to be with my Lord."

The guard returned his pistol to its holster, shaking his head in bewilderment.

Later Ivan learned that his wife and children had been praying for him on that same night as they read Isaiah 51:14: "The cowering prisoners will soon be set free; they will not die in their dungeon, nor will they lack bread" (NIV).

Ivan was released shortly thereafter and continued faithfully to preach the gospel until he died in his eighties.

∽∾

A Small Section
of the Visible Course

The house where I was born, at 52 Rue Ernest Laude in Brussels, looks exactly as it does in the picture in my mother's photo album. The old snapshot is a study in grays. The one my husband Lars took much more recently is in color. The cobblestone street is the same in both. The bricks of which the house is built turn out to be rather pink; the white marble facade of the second and third stories has not changed. They have put new shades in the two first-floor windows, and the people in the pictures are different. In the first, on the second-floor wrought-iron balcony in sunshine, stands my mother, twenty-four years old, slim and straight, with a wonderful pile of dark satiny hair. She is wearing a dark ankle-length dress with a wide white cape-collar. In the colored picture there are two cars, and near the front door, very wind-blown, stand I. How I longed to ask the present tenants to allow me to go up to the balcony, even into the kitchen where I was born.

Over sixty years have passed since I was last there. My mother had locked the front door when she turned to the Dutch lady who was her helper.

"I feel as though I've forgotten something."

Adri knew very well what it was and wondered how far my mother would get before realizing that the five-month-old baby was still upstairs, wrapped in her bunting, ready for the ocean voyage.

There was something wondrously comforting about knowing, as I stood before that unremembered house, that this is where my parents lived, where they loved, where they welcomed into their small cold-water flat the newborn sister of their son Philip. They were missionaries, working with what was then the Belgian Gospel Mission. Lars and I visited the old buildings; the little Flemish chapel where my father taught Sunday School and probably played the Steinway piano that stands there—bought by Mrs. Norton, wife of the founder of the mission (she sold her jewels to pay for it). We looked at an old photo album there with pictures of my grandparents, my great uncle, and my parents.

All of the past, I believe, is a part of God's story of each child of His—a mystery of love and sovereignty, written before the foundation of the world, never a hindrance to the task He has designed for us, but rather the very preparation suited to our particular personality's need.

"How can that be?" ask those whose heritage has not been a godly one as mine was, whose lives have not been peaceful. "It is the glory of God to conceal a matter" (Proverbs 25:2, NIV). God conceals much that we do not need to know, yet we do know that He calls His own sheep by name and leads them out. When does that begin? Does the Shepherd overlook anything that the sheep need?

William Kay, who translated the Psalms in 1870, gives this note on Psalm 73:22: "Though I was supported by Thee and living 'with Thee' as thy guest, yet I was insensible to Thy presence;—intent only on a small section of the visible course of things;—like the irrational animals that are ever looking down at the ground they are grazing.

"Yet I am perpetually with Thee, Thou hast laid hold on my right hand," wrote the psalmist. "Thou wilt guide me with Thy counsel and afterwards receive me in glory.... And as for me, nearness to God is my good; I have put my trust in the Lord God" (vv. 23, 24, 28, WK).

CRCRCD

A Lesson in Things Temporal

I am upset when things are lost. Even small things. I like to know that things have places and are in them. It's much worse when something like a manuscript is lost. I had worked for a number of weeks on a certain piece, and when I went to do the final rewriting it was gone. It just wasn't anywhere. I looked, then Lars looked, then we both looked. In all the likely and all the unlikely places. We prayed about it, of course, together and separately, but we could not find it. At last I told the Lord that if I did not find it today I would begin again from scratch, as the deadline was closing in. That day Uncle Tom, who was eighty-nine and was staying with us, became very ill. There was no time to think of manuscripts.

The next day we happened to move a piece of furniture and discovered that moths were doing their dastardly work underneath it. Lars went out and bought a can of moth spray and proceeded to fumigate every nook and cranny. The manuscript was behind a desk. It had fallen down and lodged standing up on the baseboard. If Uncle Tom had not gotten sick I would have done a day's unnecessary work on that piece that I was so worried about. If the moths had not taken it into their tiny heads to chew my carpet, we probably would not have turned up that sheaf of papers until next spring. It was not for nothing that the collect in my church that Sunday (the eighth after Pentecost) was: "O God, the protector of all who trust in you, without whom nothing is strong, nothing is holy: Increase and multiply upon us your mercy, that, with you as our ruler and guide, we may so pass through things temporal, that we lose not the things eternal; through Jesus Christ our Lord, who lives and reigns with you and the Holy Spirit, one God, for ever and ever. Amen."

Be quiet, why this anxious heed
About thy tangled ways?
God knows them all, He giveth speed,
And He allows delays.

E.W.

CRORO

Nevertheless We Must Run Aground

Have you ever put heart and soul into something, prayed over it, worked at it with a good heart because you believed it to be what God wanted, and finally seen it "run aground"?

The story of Paul's voyage as a prisoner across the Adriatic Sea tells how an angel stood beside him and told him not to be afraid (in spite of winds of hurricane force), for God would spare his life and the lives of all with him on board ship. Paul cheered his guards and fellow passengers with that word, but added, "Nevertheless, we must run aground on some island" (Acts 27:26, NIV).

It would seem that the God who promises to spare all hands might have "done the job right," saved the ship as well, and spared them the ignominy of having to make it to land on the flotsam and jetsam that was left. The fact is He did not, nor does He always spare us.

Heaven is not *here*, it's *There*. If we were given all we wanted here, our hearts would settle for this world rather than the next. God is forever luring us up and away from this one, wooing us to Himself and His still invisible Kingdom, where we will certainly find what we so keenly long for.

"Running aground," then, is not the end of the world. But it helps to make the world a bit less appealing. It may even be God's answer to "Lead us not into temptation"—the temptation complacently to settle for visible things.

There Are No Accidents

My friend Judy Squier of Portola Valley, California, is one of the most cheerful and radiant women I know. I met her first in a prayer meeting at the beginning of a conference. She was sitting in a wheel chair, and I noticed something funny about her legs. Later that day I saw her with no legs at all. In the evening she was walking around with crutches. Of course I had to ask her some questions. She was born with no legs; she had artificial ones which she used sometimes, but they were tiresome, she said (laughing) and she often left them behind. When I heard of a little baby boy named Brandon Scott, born without arms or legs, I asked if she would write to his parents. She did:

"The first thing I would say is that all that this entails is at least one hundred times harder on the parents than the child. A birth defect by God's grace does not rob childhood of its wonder, nor is a child burdened by high expectations. Given a supportive, creative, and loving family, I know personally that I enjoyed not a less-than-average life nor an average life, but as I've told many, my life has been not ordinary but extraordinary.

"I am convinced without a doubt that a loving Heavenly Father oversees the creative miracles in the inner sanctum of each mother's womb (Psalm 139), and that in His sovereignty there are no accidents.

"'What the caterpillar calls the end of the world, the Creator calls a butterfly.' As humanity we see only the imperfect, underside of God's tapestry of our lives. What we judge to be 'tragic—the most dreaded thing that could happen,' I expect we'll one day see as the awesome reason for the beauty and uniqueness of our life and our family. I think that's why James 1:2 is a favorite verse of mine. Phillips' translation put it this way: 'When all kinds of trials and temptations crowd into your lives, my brothers, don't resent them as intruders but welcome them as friends.'

"I love Joni Eareckson Tada's quote. When I saw it on the front of *Moody Monthly*, October 1982, I was convinced she'd penned the words for my epitaph. Now my husband David is aghast to hear me say I want it on my tombstone! Glory be!

> People with disabilities are God's best visual aids to demonstrate who He really is. His power shows up best in weakness. And who by the world's standards is weaker than the mentally or physically disabled? As the world watches, these people persevere. They live, love, trust and obey Him. Eventually the world is forced to say, "How great their God must be to inspire this kind of loyalty."

"Being Christian didn't shield my family from the pain and tears that came with my birth defect. In fact, ten years ago when David and I interviewed our parents for a Keepsake Tape, I was stunned to hear my mother's true feelings. I asked her to tell the hardest thing in her life. Her response: 'the day Judy Ann was born and it still is....' And yet when we as a family look back over the years, our reflections are invariably silenced by the *wonder* of God's handiwork. Someday I hope to put it in a book and I *know* it will be to the glory of God.

"Getting married and becoming a mother were dreams I never dared to dream, but God, the doer of *all* miracles intended that my life be blessed with an incredible husband and three daughters. Emily is nine, Betsy will soon be seven, and Naphtalie Joy is four. I've decided that every handicapped person needs at least one child. They are fantastic helpers and so willing to let me 'borrow their legs' when I need help.

"You as a family have been chosen in a special way to display His unique Masterwork. I pray that your roots of faith will grow deep down into the faithfulness of God's Loving Plan, that you will exchange your inadequacy for the Adequacy of Jesus' resurrection power, and that you will be awed as you witness the fruits of the Spirit manifested in your family."

Learning the Father's Love

When my brother Dave was very small, we spent a week at the seaside in Belmar, New Jersey. In vain my father tried to persuade the little boy to come into the waves with him and jump, promising to hold him safely and not allow the waves to sweep over his head. He took me (only a year older) into the ocean and showed Dave how much fun it would be. Nothing doing. The ocean was terrifying. Dave was sure it would mean certain disaster, and he could not trust his father. On the last day of our vacation he gave in. He was not swept away, his father held him as promised, and he had far more fun than he could have imagined, whereupon he burst into tears and wailed, "Why didn't you *make* me go in?"

An early lesson in prayer often comes through an ordeal of fear. We face impending adversity and we doubt the love, wisdom and power of our Father in heaven. We've tried everything else and in our desperation we turn to prayer—of the primitive sort: here's Somebody who's reputed to be able to do anything. The great question is, can I get Him to do what I want? How do I twist His arm, how persuade a remote and reluctant deity to change His mind?

When the people of Israel were encamped in Pi-hahiroth and saw the Egyptians coming after them, they felt they were looking death in the face and it was all Moses' fault—"as if there weren't enough graves in Egypt that you brought us out here to die!"

"Don't be afraid," said Moses. "Stand by. The Lord will fight for you if you'll just be quiet."

You know the story of deliverance—the sea was rolled back,

Israel marched through it dry shod, and when the Egyptians pursued them the sea swamped their horses, their chariots, and the whole army. "Not even one of them remained." The song of victory Moses and Israel sang reveals their recognition not only of the strength, majesty and wonder-working of the Lord, but of His loving-kindness, immeasurably beyond anything they had dared to hope.

Poor Dave! His father could have forced him to come into the water, but he could not have forced him to relax and enjoy it. As long as the child insisted on protecting himself, saving the life he was sure he would lose, he could not trust the strong love of his father. He refused to surrender. In this simple story we hear echoes of the most ancient story, of the two who, distrusting the word of their Father, fearing that obedience to Him would ultimately bar them from happiness, chose to repudiate their dependence on Him. Sin, death, destruction for the whole race were the result.

Learning to pray is learning to trust the wisdom, the power, and the love of our Heavenly Father, always so far beyond our dreams. He knows our need and knows ways to meet it that have never entered our heads. Things we feel sure we need for happiness may often lead to our ruin. Things we think will ruin us (the chariots of Egypt, the waters of the sea, or the little waves in Belmar!), if we believe what the Father tells us and surrender ourselves into His strong arms, bring us deliverance and joy.

The only escape from self-love is self-surrender. "Whoever loses his life for Me will find it" (Matthew 16:25, NIV). "Dwell in my love. If you heed my commands, you will dwell in my love, as I have heeded my Father's commands and dwell in His love. I have spoken thus to you, so that my joy may be in you, and your joy complete" (John 15:9-11, NEB). My father knew far better than his small, fearful, stubborn son what would give him joy. So does our Heavenly Father. Whenever I have resisted Him, I have cheated myself, as my little brother did. Whenever I have yielded, I have found joy.

A Lighthouse
in Brooklyn

For forty years a little piece of my heart has been in Brooklyn, New York. For a few months in 1951 I lived there in order to attend a Spanish-speaking church and take language lessons before going to Ecuador. But now a bigger piece of my heart is in Brooklyn—so big, in fact, that I have felt a longing to give up the house we live in and the work we do and just *move* there!

I'll explain. I'd been invited to speak to a group of women on a Saturday afternoon at Brooklyn Tabernacle. It sounded interesting, but I was not expecting anything quite so thrilling as it proved to be. Brooklyn, for a start, is a tough place. There's a lot of poverty. Drugs and muggings and murders are practically everyday occurrences, and there had been some very ugly riots between Jews and blacks in one of the most "civilized" sections. The neighborhood where I had lived was pretty bleak back then, so I wondered if it could be any worse now. I was eager to try to find 519 Bushwick Avenue (a fifth-floor walk-up, at $17 per month—lots of noise, strange cooking odors, large rats, and very little heat or hot water). Abraham, the kind man who drove us around, managed to find the location all right, but the whole block had been razed (no wonder). There was nothing there but empty lots. Well, not empty really— mattresses, old refrigerators, bedsprings, tires, sofas with the stuffings coming out—you name it, you could have picked it up. In fact, there were such mountains of trash everywhere, I wondered where they'd put it if they ever *did* decide to clean up the place.

Desolate and depressing in the extreme. Graffiti, that hideous evidence of defiance of all law and order, covered every surface within reach of the ground and many high above it. Abraham said thousands of people are always cleaning it up, and it's back the next morning.

I kept thinking about the old gospel song, "Let the Lower Lights Be Burning." Here's part of it:

Dark the night of sin has settled,
Loud the angry billows roar;
Eager eyes are watching, longing,
For the lights along the shore.

Let the lower lights be burning,
Send a gleam across the wave,
Some poor, fainting, struggling seaman
You may rescue, you may save.

There on Flatbush Avenue stands Brooklyn Tabernacle, sending its gleam across the wave. Thousands have "made the harbor" because of its light. My audience was a wonderful mixture of colors and ethnic backgrounds, the music was louder than I'm used to but wonderfully exuberant and heartfelt. There was no doubt about it—those women were *worshipping*. I heard some of their stories—to me nearly unimaginable—of drugs, alcohol, abuse, poverty, abandonment. One mother's anonymous letter to the pastor told of her own heartbreak. Just that week she had learned that her fourteen-year-old daughter was pregnant. The father of the baby was the girl's seventeen-year-old brother. That mother said she had wanted to kill herself and her children, "But I'm making it," she wrote, "with Jesus and the help of this church."

We heard their two-hundred-voice choir at the Billy Graham rally in Central Park on Sunday afternoon. In the evening, after I had spoken again at the Tabernacle, we were having supper with a group of the church folks. I asked a woman named Marie to tell me her story. Her husband smiled and said, "She loves to tell it! It's her favorite story." How I wish I had room for the whole thing.

Her mother, five months pregnant, died of cancer. Marie, the baby, survived and was put in a foundling hospital. Later she was entrusted to the care of nuns who treated her cruelly, although they taught her about God. She felt sure God was better than they were, and she knew her daddy loved her, but she was hungry for more. At age ten she began sniffing glue. This led to smoking pot, then doing drugs for the next fifteen years. On a Club Med vacation in Mexico with her boyfriend she began to wonder why she was born. Why had God made her? What meaning was there in it all? God clearly spoke to her "Maria, give me your life. This is your last chance." Suddenly she lost her desire for drugs and told her boyfriend she would not sleep with him anymore. On her return to New York she found that a group of friends had been praying for her at the very time when this happened. Hers is a totally transformed life. She's married to the boyfriend, who is now a pastor.

"You should have seen *me*," he said, "long hair, three earrings in each ear, feathers!"

I thought of my own upbringing—Christ as the Head of our house, parents who loved Him, each other, and us. No alcohol or drugs, just the Bible and hymn-singing. A clean house on a clean street. I thought of Nicky Cruz's testimony that same afternoon at the Graham meeting—from deep sin and sorrow to joy; and of Johnny Cash's simple words: "Alcohol never gave me peace. Drugs never brought me happiness. I found both in Jesus Christ. He changed my life." Then he sang, "The Old Account Was Settled Long Ago," while his dear June burst in with her lusty refrain, "Down on my knees!"

Tears come as I write, remembering the unutterable JOY I saw on those upturned faces during those two days. Those people were still living with huge tribulations and deep heartbreaks, yet there was joy, there was peace, and there was love such as I see in few churches. I don't know when I've had so many hugs. How to account for it all? It's quite simple:

This doctrine of the cross is sheer folly to those on their way to ruin, but to us who are on the way to salvation, it is the power of God.... To shame the wise, God has chosen what the world counts folly, and to shame what is strong, God has chosen what the world counts weakness. He has chosen things low and contemptible, mere nothings, to overthrow the existing order. So there is no place for human pride in the presence of God.... He is our righteousness; in him we are consecrated and set free.

1 Corinthians 1:18, 27-30, NEB

Does God Allow His Children to Be Poor?

God allows both Christians and non-Christians to experience every form of suffering known to the human race, just as He allows His blessings to fall on both. Poverty, like other forms of suffering, is relative, as Lars and I were reminded while we were in India. Our country's definition of the "poverty level" would mean unimaginable affluence to the girls we saw working next to our hotel. For nine hours a day they carried wet concrete in wooden basins on their heads, pouring it into the forms for the foundation of a large building. They were paid thirty cents a day.

On my list of Scriptures which give clues to some of God's reasons for allowing His children to suffer is 2 Corinthians 8:2: "Somehow, in most difficult circumstances, their joy and the fact of being down to their last penny themselves, produced a magnificent concern for other people" (PHILLIPS). It was the Macedonian churches that Paul was talking about, living proof that it is not poverty or riches that determine generosity, and sometimes those who suffer the most financially are the ones most ready to share what they have. "They simply begged us to accept their gifts and so let them share the honors of supporting their brothers in Christ" (v. 4).

Money holds terrible power when it is loved. It can blind us, shackle us, fill us with anxiety and fear, torment our days and nights with misery, wear us out with chasing it. The Macedonian Christians, possessing little of it, accepted their lot with faith and trust. Their eyes were opened to see past their own misery. They saw what mattered far more than a bank account, and, out of "magnificent concern," contributed to the needs of their brothers.

If through losing what this world prizes we are enabled to gain what it despises—treasure in heaven, invisible and incorruptible—isn't it worth any kind of suffering? What is it worth to us to learn a little bit more of what the Cross means—life out of death, the transformation of earth's losses and heartbreaks and tragedies?

Poverty has not been my experience, but God has allowed in the lives of each of us some sort of loss, the withdrawal of something we valued, in order that we may learn to offer ourselves a little more willingly, to allow the touch of death on one more thing we have clutched so tightly, and thus know fullness and freedom and joy that much sooner. We're not naturally inclined to love God and seek His Kingdom. Trouble may help to incline us—that is, it may tip us over, put some pressure on us, lean us in the right direction.

Why Is God Doing This to Me?

An article appeared in the *National Geographic* years ago which has affected my thinking ever since. "The Incredible Universe," by Kenneth F. Weaver and James P. Blair, included this paragraph:

> How can the human mind deal with the knowledge that the farthest object we can see in the universe is perhaps ten billion light years away! Imagine that the thickness of this page represents the distance from the earth to the sun (93,000,000 miles, or about eight light minutes). Then the distance to the nearest star (4-1/3 light years) is a 71-foot-high stack of paper. And the diameter of our own galaxy (100,000 light years) is a 310-mile stack, while the edge of the known universe is not reached until the pile of paper is 31,000,000 miles high, a third of the way to the sun.

Thirty-one million miles. That's a very big stack of paper. By the time I get to thirty-one-and-a-half million I'm lost—aren't you? I read somewhere else that our galaxy is one (only one) of perhaps ten billion.

I know the One who made all that. He is my Shepherd. This is what He says: "With my own hands I founded the earth, with my right hand I formed the expanse of sky; when I summoned them, they sprang at once into being.... I teach you for your own advantage and lead you in the way you must go. If only you had listened to my commands, your prosperity would have rolled on like a river in flood... (Isaiah 48:13, 17, 18, NEB).

Hardly a day goes by without my receiving a letter, a phone call, or a visit from someone in trouble. Almost always the question comes, in one form or another, *Why does God do this to me?*

When I am tempted to ask that same question, it loses its power when I remember that this Lord, into whose strong hands I long ago committed my life, is engineering a universe of unimaginable proportions and complexity. How could I possibly understand all that He must take into consideration as He deals with it and with me, a single individual! He has given us countless assurances that we cannot get lost in the shuffle. He choreographs the "molecular dance" which goes on every second of every minute of every day in every cell in the universe. For the record, *one* cell has about 200 trillion molecules. He makes note of the smallest seed and the tiniest sparrow. He is not too busy to keep records even of my falling hair.

Yet in our darkness we suppose He has overlooked us. He hasn't. I have been compiling a list of the answers God Himself has given us to our persistent question about adversity:

1. We need to be pruned. In Jesus' last discourse with His disciples before He was crucified (a discourse meant for us as well as for them), He explained that God is the gardener, He Himself is the vine, and we are branches. If we are bearing fruit, then we must be pruned. This is a painful process. Jesus knew that His disciples would face much suffering. He showed them, in this beautiful metaphor, that it was not for nothing. Only the well-pruned vine bears the best fruit. They could take comfort in knowing that the pruning proved they were neither barren nor withered, for in that case they would simply be burned up in the brushpile.

Pruning requires the cutting away not only of what is superfluous but also of what appears to be good stock. Why should we be so baffled when the Lord cuts away good things from our lives? He has explained why. "This is my Father's glory, that you may bear fruit in plenty and so be my disciples" (John 15:8, NEB). We need not see *how* it works. He has told us it *does* work.

2. We need to be refined. Peter wrote to God's scattered people, reminding them that even though they were "smarting for a little while under trials of many kinds" (they were in exile—the sort of trial most of us would think rather more than a "smart"), they were nevertheless *chosen* in the purpose of God, *hallowed* to His service, and *consecrated* with the blood of Jesus Christ. With all that, they still needed refining. Gold is gold, but it has to go through fire. Faith is even more precious, so faith will always have another test to stand. Remember God's loving promise of 2 Corinthians 12:9, "My grace is all you need; power comes to its full strength in weakness" (NEB).

> But Thou art making me, I thank Thee, sire.
> What Thou hast done and doest Thou knows't well.
> And I will help Thee; gently in Thy fire
> I will lie burning; on Thy potter's wheel
> I will whirl patient, though my brain should reel.
> Thy grace shall be enough the grief to quell,
> And growing strength perfect through weakness dire.

George MacDonald
Diary of an Old Soul, October 2

How shalt thou bear the cross that now
So dread a weight appears?
Keep quietly to God, and think
Upon the Eternal Years.

E.W. Faber

CRORD

Ever Been Bitter?

Sometimes I've said, "O Lord, you wouldn't do this to me, would you? How could you, Lord?" I can recall such times later on and realize that my perspective was skewed. One Scripture passage which helps me rectify it is Isaiah 45:9-11 (NEB): "Will the pot contend with the potter, or the earthenware with the hand that shapes it? Will the clay ask the potter what he is making?... Thus says the Lord, would you dare question me concerning my children, or instruct me in my handiwork? I alone, I made the earth and created man upon it." He knows exactly what He is doing. I am *clay*. The word humble comes from the root word *humus*, earth, clay. Let me remember that when I question God's dealings. I don't understand Him, but then I'm not asked to understand, only to trust. Bitterness dissolves when I remember the kind of love with which He has loved me—He gave Himself for me. He gave Himself for me. *He gave Himself for me.* Whatever He is doing now, therefore, is not cause for bitterness. It has to be designed for good, because He loved me and gave Himself for me.

Is it a sin to ask God why?

It is always best to go first for our answers to Jesus Himself. He cried out on the cross, "My God, my God, why have You forsaken me?" It was a human cry, a cry of desperation, springing from His heart's agony at the prospect of being put into the hands of wicked men and actually *becoming sin* for you and me. We can never suffer anything like that, yet we do at times feel forsaken and cry, *Why, Lord?*

The psalmist asked why. Job, a blameless man, suffering horri-

ble torments on an ash heap, asked why. It does not seem to me to
be sinful to ask the question. What is sinful is resentment against
God and His dealings with us. When we begin to doubt His love
and imagine that He is cheating us of something we have a right
to, we are guilty as Adam and Eve were guilty. They took the
snake at his word rather than God. The same snake comes to us
repeatedly with the same suggestions: Does God love you? Does
He really want the best for you? Is His word trustworthy? Isn't He
cheating you? Forget His promises. You'd be better off if you do it
your way.

I have often asked why. Many things have happened which I
didn't plan on and which human rationality could not explain. In
the darkness of my perplexity and sorrow I have heard Him say
quietly, *Trust Me.* He knew that my question was not the challenge of unbelief or resentment. I have never doubted that He
loves me, but I have sometimes felt like St. Teresa of Avila who,
when she was dumped out of a carriage into a ditch, said, "If this is
the way You treat your friends, no wonder You have so few!" Job
was not, it seems to me, a very patient man. But he never gave up
his conviction that he was in God's hands. God was big enough to
take whatever Job dished out (see Job 16 for a sample). Do not be
afraid to tell Him exactly how you feel (He's already read your
thoughts anyway). Don't tell the whole world. God can take it—
others can't. Then listen for His answer. Six scriptural answers to
the question WHY come from: 1 Peter 4:12-13; Romans 5:3-4; 2
Corinthians 12:9; John 14:31; Romans 8:17; Colossians 1:24. There
is mystery, but it is not all mystery. Here are clear reasons.

∞∞∞

Lord, Please Remove the Dilemma

Because my husband Lars is a Norwegian who would happily eat fish three times a day if I'd give it to him (I seldom do), I often have fishheads and fishbones to discard. I don't like the noise the disposal makes if I put them in there, so I fire them out the window onto the grass. A prompt and thorough garbage service is provided free of charge by the seven resident crows who materialize out of nowhere (nine minutes is the maximum time it has taken them to detect my offerings). Recently I watched one of them attempt to stuff all the pieces into his beak before his buddies had arrived. He carefully picked up everything except one long backbone. Here was a dilemma. How was he to grab the backbone without dropping the beakful he already had? Solemnly he surveyed the scene, stepped slowly around the bone and cogitated. So everything is done by instinct, is it? I don't believe it. He was reasoning. He made a decision. He dropped the smaller pieces, grasped the bone right in the middle and raised it. Too unwieldy. More cogitation. Then, delicately, he lifted one end of the backbone, bent it around with his claw and picked up the other end. Now, holding both ends in his beak he succeeded somehow (I couldn't for the life of me see exactly how) in gathering all but a few small bits and flew off, triumphant, to relish his find in solitude.

Is there anyone reading this who is not faced with a perplexity of some sort? Some of you face serious dilemmas. We want to pray,

"Lord, please remove the dilemma." Usually the answer is "No, not right away." We must face it, pray over it, think about it, wait on the Lord, make a choice. Sometimes it is an excruciating choice.

St. Augustine said, "The very pleasures of human life men acquire by difficulties." There are times when the entire arrangement of our existence is disrupted and we long then for just one ordinary day—seeing our ordinary life as greatly desirable, even wonderful, in the light of the terrible disruption that has taken place. Difficulty opens our eyes to pleasures we had taken for granted.

I recall one of the times my second husband Add was released from the hospital when he had cancer. I did not suppose he was cured, but just having him at home once more was all I asked for that day. I set the table in the dining room with candlelight as I always did for dinner. I had fixed his favorite meal—steak, baked potato, salad, my homebaked apple pie. As he bowed his head to give thanks in the usual way, I had a sudden urge to do something very unusual—to drop to the floor and clutch his hands and sing "Let us break bread together on our knees." I didn't do it. Things proceeded in the ordinary way, but there was a new radiance about them simply because we had been deprived for a while, and knew we would soon be deprived again, probably permanently.

Paul said he had been "very thoroughly initiated into the human lot with all its ups and downs" (Philippians 4:12, NEB). He was hard-pressed, bewildered, persecuted, and struck down. God in His mercy did not choose to remove the dilemmas with which he was faced (some of His greatest mercies are His refusals), but chose instead to make Himself known to Paul *because* of them, in ways which would strengthen his faith and make him a strengthener and an instrument of peace to the rest of us. Hard-pressed he was, but not hemmed in—God promises that none of us will ever be tempted beyond our power to endure. Bewildered he was, but *never* at wit's end—God promises wisdom to those who ask for it. Persecuted, but never left to "stand it alone"—God promises His unfailing presence, all the days of our lives. Struck down, Paul was not left to die, though some of his rescues were ignominious in the extreme—the great apostle, let down over a wall in a basket, and on occasion making it to land on a chunk of flotsam! Hardly the means he would have envisioned God's using to fulfill His promises. But on second thought, why not? The absurdity of it all does us good. Life is absurd—on the surface of things—but every bit of it is planned, as Paul goes on to say:

"It is for your sake that all things are ordered, so that, as the abounding grace of God is shared by more and more, the greater may be the chorus of thanksgiving that ascends to the glory of God" (2 Corinthians 4:15, NEB). Maybe Paul's testimony, which has cheered countless millions, will cheer somebody who still faces a dilemma he has begged the Lord to remove. All of Paul's were solved, but not all of them in Paul's way or Paul's time, *Selah.*

$\infty\infty$

Maybe This Year...?

"I hardly know where to start," a letter begins. "My story is not one involving men. That's the problem. Male companionship seems not to be found, and, I fear, may never be found. They never ask me out twice. I'm always 'dumped.' The problem is *I want a relationship.* I have this overwhelming desire...."

Someone else said to me, "I fell deeply in love. He fell deeply in love, too—with someone else."

Another letter tells of the agonized yearning of one couple for a child. Since God has not removed the desire, they ask, may we not conclude that He wants us to employ whatever means we can (e.g., *in vitro* fertilization) in order to have a child?

God's not having taken away a perfectly normal human desire does not by any means indicate that we are free to pursue its fulfillment in any way we choose. A woman who had, after years of struggles, quickly lost sixty pounds told me that she had been expecting *God* to take away her appetite. When she realized He did not intend to do so (she had been asking for the removal of our God-given protection from starvation!), she stopped gratifying that appetite in the wrong ways.

Will the young woman find a mate? Will the couple have a child? Maybe this year will be the year of desire fulfilled. Perhaps, on the other hand, it will be the year of desire radically transformed, the year of finding, as we have perhaps not yet truly found, Christ to be the All-Sufficient One, Christ the "deep, sweet well of Love."

"Why won't God let someone into my life? I feel left out, abandoned. *When* will it be my turn?" The petulant letter goes on. "I feel deprived! Will He deny me the one small desire of my heart? Is it too big a treasure to ask? I sit in torture and dismay."

Life is likely to continue to hold many forms of torture and dismay for that unhappy person and for all who refuse to receive with thanksgiving instead of complaint the place in life God has chosen for them. The torture is self-inflicted, for God has not rejected their prayers. He knows better than any of us do what furthers our salvation. Our true happiness is to be realized precisely *through* his refusals, which are always *mercies.* His choice is flawlessly contrived to give the deepest kind of joy as soon as it is embraced.

Joseph Eliot, in the seventeenth century, said, "I need everything God gives me, and want [or feel the lack of] nothing He denies me."

In Moses' review of God's leading of the children of Israel he said,

> Remember how the Lord your God led you all the way in the desert these forty years, to humble you and to test you in order to know what was in your heart.... He humbled you, *causing* you to hunger and then fed you with manna which neither you nor your fathers had known, to *teach* you that man does not live on bread alone but on every word that comes from the mouth of the Lord.... Know then in your heart that as a man disciplines his son, so the Lord your God disciplines you.... For the Lord your God is bringing you into a good land—a land with streams and pools of water, with springs flowing in the valleys and hills; a land with wheat and barley, vines and fig trees, pomegranates, olive oil and honey; a land where bread will not be scarce and you will lack nothing.
>
> **Deuteronomy 8:2-3, 5, 7-9, NIV (emphasis added)**

The cause of our discontent: We simply do not *believe* God. The wilderness experience leads to the Promised Land. It is the path God chose for us. His Word is established forever, and He tells us in a thousand ways that His will is our peace, His choices for us will lead to fulfillment and joy, the way of transgressors is hard. Do we suppose that *we* could find a better way than His?

One of George Eliot's characters says:

> You are seeking your own will, my daughter. You are seeking some good other than the law you are bound to obey. But how will you find good? It is not a thing of choice; it is a river that flows from the foot of the Invisible Throne, and flows by the path of obedience. I say again, man cannot choose his duties. You may choose to forsake your duties, and choose not to have the sorrow they bring. But you will go forth, and what will you find, my daughter? Sorrow without duty—bitter herbs, and no bread with them.

Instead of seeing His everlasting love, tenderly bending down to our humanness, longing over each one of us with a father's speechless longing, we sometimes think of Him as indifferent, inaccessible, or just plain unfair.

The worst pains we experience are not those of the suffering itself but of our stubborn resistance to it, our resolute insistence on our independence. To be "crucified with Christ" means what Oswald Chambers calls "breaking the husk" of that independence. "Has that break come?" he asks. "All the rest is pious fraud." And you and I know, in our heart of hearts, that that sword-thrust (so typical of Chambers!) is the straight truth.

If we reject *this* cross, we will not find it in this world again. *Here* is the opportunity offered. Be patient. Wait on the Lord for whatever He appoints, wait quietly, wait trustingly. He holds every minute of every hour of every day of every week of every month of every year in His hands. Thank Him in advance for what the future holds, for He is already *there*. "Lord, you have assigned me my portion and my cup" (Psalm 16:5, NIV). Shall we not gladly say, "I'll take it, Lord! YES! I'll trust you for everything. Bless the Lord, O my soul!"

I've many a cross to take up now,
And many left behind;
But present troubles move me not,
Nor shake my quiet mind.
And what may be to-morrow's cross
I never seek to find;
My Father says, "Leave that to me,
And keep a quiet mind."

Anonymous

Do Not Forecast Grief

Sitting one still and sunny afternoon in a tiny chapel on an island in the South, I thought I heard someone enter. A young woman was weeping quietly. After a little time I asked if I could help. She confided her fears for the future—what if her husband should die? Or one of her children? What if money ran out?

All our fears represent in some form, I believe, the fear of death, common to all of us. But is it our business to pry into what may happen tomorrow? It is a difficult and painful exercise which saps the strength and uses up the time given us *today*. Once we give ourselves up to God, shall we attempt to get hold of what can never belong to us—*tomorrow*? Our lives are His, our times in His hand, He is Lord over what *will* happen, never mind what *may* happen. When we prayed "Thy will be done," did we suppose He did not hear us? He heard indeed, and daily makes our business His and partakes of our lives. If my life is once surrendered, all is well. Let me not grab it back, as though it were in peril in *His* hand but would be safer in *mine!*

Today is mine. Tomorrow is none of my business. If I peer anxiously into the fog of the future, I will strain my spiritual eyes so that I will not see clearly what is required of me now.

"Sufficient unto the day is the evil thereof"—and the work thereof. The evil is not a part of the yoke Jesus asks us to take. Our work is, and He takes that yoke with us. I will overextend myself if I assume anything more.

God chains the dog till night; wilt loose the chain
And wake thy sorrow?
Wilt thou forestall it, and now grieve tomorrow,
And then again
Grieve over freshly all thy pain?

Either grief will not come, or if it must,
Do not forecast;
And while it cometh, it is almost past.
Away, distrust;
My God hath promis'd; He is just.

George Herbert, "The Discharge"

∽∽∽

How Long Is God's Arm?

How do we reconcile God's promises for protection with the fact that so many evil things do happen in our lives? Can we believe God for protection?

This question comes up often, and no wonder, since there are many promises in the Bible about protection, including (especially in the Old Testament) physical protection. We must be careful to interpret Scripture with Scripture, and if we examine the record we find that God did not by any means always protect His people from harm. He has absolute power to keep us safe, both physically and spiritually, but His engineering of the universe made room for man's freedom to choose—that is, freedom to will to obey or to disobey Him. This is a deep mystery. Man's disobedience brought evil into the world, and all of us are subject to it. God does not cancel out its effects, even for His choicest servants (John the Baptist, Stephen, those nameless victims of Hebrews 11:35-37, for example).

Nevertheless, we have the promises. Romans 8:35-39 is one of my most reread passages. I believe we can rest assured that we are invulnerable so long as God does not give permission for us to be hurt. If He gives that permission, He will not leave us alone. He goes with us through the valley, the deep water, the furnace. He will never, absolutely never, leave us or forsake us.

∽∽∽

There is No Other Way

In order to get to a place called Laity Lodge in Texas you have to drive into a riverbed. The road takes you down a steep, rocky hill into a canyon and straight into the water. There is a sign at the water's edge which says, "Yes. You drive in the river."

One who has made up his mind to go to the uttermost with God will come to a place as unexpected and perhaps looking as impossible to travel as that riverbed looks. He may glance around for an alternative route, but if he wants what God promises His faithful ones, he must go straight into the danger. There is no other way.

The written word is our direction. Trust it. Obey it. Drive in the river and get to Laity Lodge. Moses said to Israel, "I offer you the choice of life or death, blessing or curse. Choose life and then you and your descendants will live; love the Lord your God, obey him, and hold fast to him: that is life for you."

When you take the risk of obedience, you find solid rock beneath you—and markers, evidence that someone has traveled this route before. "The Lord your God will cross over at your head... he will be with you; he will not fail you or forsake you. Do not be discouraged or afraid" (Deuteronomy 30:19, 20; 31:3, 8, NEB). It's what the old gospel song puts so simply:

Trust and obey, for there's no other way
To be happy in Jesus but to trust and obey.

John H. Sammis

cococo

Moonless Trust

Some of you are perhaps feeling that you are voyaging just now on a moonless sea. Uncertainty surrounds you. There seem to be no signs to follow. Perhaps you feel about to be engulfed by loneliness. There is no one to whom you can speak of your need. Amy Carmichael wrote of such a feeling when, as a missionary of twenty-six, she had to leave Japan because of poor health, then travel to China for recuperation, but then realized God was telling her to go to Ceylon. (All this preceded her going to India, where she stayed for fifty-three years.) I have on my desk her original handwritten letter of August 25, 1894, as she was en route to Colombo. "All along, let us remember, we are not asked to understand, but simply to obey.... On July 28, Saturday, I sailed. We had to come on board on Friday night, and just as the tender (a small boat) where were the dear friends who had come to say goodbye was moving off, and the chill of loneliness shivered through me, like a warm love-clasp came the long-loved lines—'And only Heaven is better than to walk with Christ at midnight, over moonless seas.' I couldn't feel frightened then. Praise Him for the moonless seas—all the better the opportunity for proving Him to be indeed the El Shaddai, 'the God who is Enough.'"

Let me add my own word of witness to hers and to that of the tens of thousands who have learned that He is indeed Enough. He is not all we would ask for (if we were honest), but it is precisely when we do not have what we would ask for, and *only then*, that we can clearly perceive His all-sufficiency. It is when the sea is moonless that the Lord has become my Light.

∽∽∽

Don't Forfeit Your Peace

It would not be possible to exaggerate the importance hymns and spiritual songs have played in my spiritual growth. One of the latter, familiar to most of you, has this line: "O what peace we often forfeit, O what needless pain we bear, all because we do not carry everything to God in prayer" (Joseph Scriven). Prayerlessness is one of many ways by which we can easily forfeit the peace God wants us to have. I've been thinking of some other ways. Here's a sampling:

1. Resent God's ways.
2. Worry as much as possible.
3. Pray only about things you can't manage by yourself.
4. Refuse to accept what God gives.
5. Look for peace elsewhere than in Him.
6. Try to rule your own life.
7. Doubt God's word.
8. Carry all your cares.

If you'd rather *not* forfeit your peace, here are eight ways to find it (antidotes to the above eight):

1. "Great peace have they which love thy law: and nothing shall offend them" (Psalm 119:165 KJV). "Circumstances are the expression of God's will," wrote Bishop Handley Moule.

2. "Don't worry about anything whatever" (Philippians 4:6, PHILLIPS).

3. "In everything make your requests known to God in prayer and petition with thanksgiving. Then the peace of God... will guard your hearts" (Philippians 4:6,7, NEB).

4. "Take my yoke upon you and learn from me... and you will find rest" (Matthew 11:29, NIV).

5. "Peace is my parting gift to you, my own peace, such as the world cannot give" (John 14:27, NEB).

6. "Let the peace of Christ rule in your hearts" (Colossians 3:15, NIV).

7. "May the God of hope fill you with all joy and peace in believing" (Romans 15:13, KJV).

8. "Cast all your cares on him for you are his charge" (1 Peter 5:7, NEB).

Grant, O Lord my God, that I may never fall away in success or in failure; that I may not be prideful in prosperity nor dejected in adversity. Let me rejoice only in what unites us and sorrow only in what separates us. May I strive to please no one or fear to displease anyone except Yourself. May I seek always the things that are eternal and never those that are only temporal. May I shun any joy that is without You and never seek any that is beside You. O Lord, may I delight in any work I do for You and tire of any rest that is apart from You. My God, let me direct my heart towards You, and in my failings, always repent with a purpose of amendment.
St. Thomas Aquinas

A Tiny Treasure
in Heaven

One December I spent two weeks in a hotel within walking distance of my daughter Valerie's home in Mission Viejo, California. This gave me the chance to have uninterrupted writing time for mornings and early afternoons, then spend the rest of the day with her family. Four of the children thought it a wonderful lark to spend a night in the hotel with me (one of the six is too young, one too old). What pleasure for me to watch and listen and savor the marvel of each dear unfolding personality.

Early on the morning of December 4, as six-year-old Jim and four-year-old Colleen were still sleeping the sleep of the carefree and innocent (how utterly relaxed little children can be!), I was going over various matters with the Lord. Finding myself a bit anxious about a few of them, I turned to Philippians 4:5-7: "The Lord is near. Do not be anxious about anything, but in everything, by prayer and petition, with thanksgiving, present your requests to God. And the peace of God, which transcends all understanding, will guard your hearts and your minds in Christ Jesus." Copying the words into my journal helps me to obey them on the spot, so that's what I did. At seven o'clock Val called. Could I come over as soon as possible? She needed to see her doctor. We lost no time.

Later that morning when she and Walt came home I saw that she was crying. The baby she was carrying (perhaps in her fourth month) had died. Two days later, following the agonies of induced labor (much worse than I had imagined), she gave birth to a tiny girl whom they named Joy. I held her in my hand—perfectly formed, the fingers and toes about the size of hyphens. I could not help but think of the millions of babies this size who have been purposefully destroyed and cast out as "hospital waste."

The Shepard family grieved. There was no question that Joy was one of God's little lambs. The children hung a tiny stocking on the mantelpiece along with theirs. They now have a new treasure in heaven, known and loved and cared for by the Lord. Someday they will know her too. "Where your treasure is, there will your heart be." Walt and Valerie found peace in the only place it is to be found—acceptance—and were greatly comforted by the words of Philippians 3:10: "I want to know Christ and the power of his resurrection and the fellowship of sharing in his sufferings, becoming like him in his death" (NIV).

Those last six words embody, I think, what Jesus meant when He said His followers must take up the cross. Other translations: "growing conformity with his death," "reproducing the pattern of his death," "even to die as he died." How did He die? In utter self-abandonment to the Father's will. Valerie was also comforted, she told me, by the reading for that day, December 5, in *Joy and Strength* (World Wide Publications, Minneapolis, 1986):

Whatever thy grief or trouble be, take every drop in thy cup from the hand of Almighty God. He with whom "the hairs of thy head are all numbered," knoweth every throb of thy brow, each hardly drawn breath, each shoot of pain, each beating of the fevered pulse, each sinking of the aching heart. Receive, then, what are trials to *thee*, not in the main only, but one by one, from His all-loving hands; thank His love for each; unite each with the sufferings of thy Redeemer; pray that He will thereby hallow them to thee. Thou wilt not know now what He thereby will work in thee; yet, day by day, shalt thou receive the impress of the likeness of the ever-blessed Son, and in thee, too, while thou knowest it not, God shall be glorified.

E.B. Pusey

What's Out There?

Time magazine once reported the discovery of the most massive object ever detected in the universe. The odd thing is nobody knows what it is. The Kitt Peak telescope picked up two quasars ("intensely bright bodies so far away that the light they emit travels for billions of years before reaching the earth") which seemed to be identical, an occurrence astronomers consider about as likely as finding two people with identical fingerprints. Something called a "gravitation lens" seemed to be bending the light (get that!) from a single quasar in such a way as to produce two identical images. Nothing astonishing about that—Einstein predicted it more than seventy years ago, and Arthur Eddington confirmed it a few years later.

The great question is just exactly *what* is acting as a gravitational lens. Whatever it is, it has to have the mass of a thousand (1,000) galaxies. If it's a black hole, it is "at least a thousand times as large as the Milky Way (which consists of hundreds of billions of stars, including the sun)." Got that? I was bemused by the statement, "Astrophysicists find it difficult to explain how so tremendous a black hole could have formed." I guess they do. They're turning over a third possibility, much too arcane for me to peer into at all, but it has to do with the Big Bang theory of the origin of the universe.

The most numbing of the facts of this story for me is that people go to such elaborate lengths to avoid mentioning one vastly prior fundamental possibility that (surely?) stares them in the face: creation.

How much faith does it take to believe in God? Less, I venture to say—a great deal less—than to believe in the Unconscious generating the Conscious, Mindlessness creating Mind, Nothing giving birth to Something.

What we know of God we have seen in His Son. He in whom we are asked to trust is Love, creative Love; thinking of us, I suppose, before He thought of gravitational lenses; giving Himself in sacrificial love long before He gave us His own breath of life—for the Lamb was slain *before the foundation of the world.*

My Lord and my God. Forgive my faithlessness.

∞∞

Love's Sacrifice
Leads to Joy

Easter, the most joyful of all Christian feast days, follows that most sorrowful of days we remember. The joy of Easter proceeds from the Cross. Without Christ's pouring out His soul to death there would have been no resurrection. We cannot know Christ and the power of His resurrection without also entering into the fellowship of His suffering.

For years I have had on the wall of my study these lines written by one Ugo Bassi: "Measure thy life by loss instead of gain.... Love's strength standeth in Love's sacrifice." Those lines epitomize the central teaching of the Lord Jesus—that life springs forth from death (see John 12:24, 15:2; Matthew 16:24,25, and other verses). They speak to the timeworn question, *Why, Lord?* I had no idea who Bassi was, nor had any of the people I know who read old stuff. A while ago my Aunt Anne turned over to me a great pile of family papers in which, to my utter delight, I discovered a thin and tattered booklet, "Sermon in the Hospital," by Ugo Bassi. Born in 1800 of an Italian father and a Greek mother, he began his noviltiate in the Order of St. Barnabas at the age of eighteen. On Sundays he took his turn at preaching in a hospital in Rome. Harriet E. H. King heard one of these sermons and put it into verse. I wish I could pass on to you the whole thing.

Bassi chose the Vineyard chapter, John 15, as his text, showing that the life of the Vine is "not of pleasure nor of ease." Almost before the flower fades the fruit begins to grow, but instead of being allowed to grow where it will, it is tied immediately to a stake, forced to draw out of the hard hillside its nourishment. When "the fair shoots begin to wind and wave in the blue air, and feel how sweet it is," along comes the gardener with pruning hooks and shears, "and strips it bare of all its innocent pride... and cuts deep and sure, unsparing for its tenderness and joy."

(I had written just that much when my phone rang. An unknown woman called to ask me what to do for her friend Sherrill, age thirty-three, mother of eight children, ages ten years to six weeks, whose husband Bill died of a heart attack last Friday. And so it happens, nearly always, that when I am writing or preparing talks, something occurs to jolt me with the question: Do you believe what you are saying? Suppose you were in this person's shoes? Is it really true? Does it apply? O Lord, YES. You are My Father, you are Sherrill's. You are also the Gardener with the shears.)

Bassi goes on to describe the vintage, when the vine bends low with the weight of the grapes, "wrought out of the long striving of its heart." But ah! the hands are ready to tear down the treasures of the grapes; the feet are there to tread them in the wine-press "until the blood-red rivers of the wine run over, and the land is full of joy. But the vine standeth stripped and desolate, having given all, and now its own dark time is come, and no man payeth back to it the comfort and the glory of its gift." Winter comes, and the vine is cut back to the very stem (I had not known, as John and Jesus and Bassi knew, how terribly drastic is the pruning process), "despoiled, disfigured, left a leafless stock, alone through all the dark days that shall come."

While the vine undergoes this death, the wine it has produced is gladdening the heart of man. Have you, perhaps, like the vine, given happiness to others, yet found yourself seemingly forsaken? Has it made you bitter? We need the paradigm of the vine, which is "not bitter for the torment undergone, not barren for the fullness yielded up.... The Vine from every living limb bleeds wine; is it the poorer for that spirit shed?" (and in this context come the lines I keep on my wall):

Measure thy life by loss instead of gain;
Not by the wine drunk but by the wine poured forth;
For love's strength standeth in love's sacrifice,
And whoso suffers most hath most to give.

Picture the young monk, standing at the point where five long wards, lined with suffering people, converged. Even those who could not see him felt his presence as he looked down the rows of beds, heard "the sweet voice that spoke this sermon to them tenderly."

I think you will understand why the following lines spoke especially to me, who have known very little of physical pain:

I, in the midst of those who suffer so
—who needs must somewhat share the daily pain
which each of ye, Beloved, must endure,
must also seek some comfort, and some strength
of hope to live and suffer by;—and this
hath God given me, Beloved, for your sakes,
to whom I fain would pass it. Bear with me,
while unto each I seem to speak—all ye
who suffer;—and I see around me
none but suffers, but to whom, with reverence,
these words of mine, these hopes of mine, are due."

When I wrote my book *A Path through Suffering* I had not found this Sermon, but those words would have made a fitting opener.

Why is it that we do not seem to listen for God's voice except when we are in trouble? God speaks to us sometimes, Bassi says, through soft summer air, but we do not feel it to be God—only the wind. He speaks to us "when friends meet happily and all is merry," but we see only our friends. When a bird's song moves us to sudden rapture, do we hear God's voice or only the bird's? "But when the sharp strokes flesh and heart run through for thee and not another," then we know what no one else in all the universe can feel or know—the "hidden, tortured nerves," the "incommunicable pain."

God speaks Himself to us, as mothers speak
To their own babes, upon the tender flesh
With fond familiar touches close and dear;—
Because *He cannot choose a softer* way
To make us feel that He Himself is near,
And each apart His own Beloved and known" (italics mine).

Does anyone read these words who can't sleep well? Bassi writes, "He gives His angels charge of those who sleep,/But He Himself watches with those who wake." He reminds us that the Son of God was made "'perfect through suffering,' our salvation's seal set in the front of His Humanity." He was the Man of Sorrows, "and the Cross of Christ is more to us than all His miracles."

But if, impatient, thou let slip thy cross,
Thou wilt not find it in this world again,
Nor in another; here, and here alone,
Is given thee to *suffer* for God's sake.
In other worlds we shall more perfectly
Serve Him and love Him, praise Him, work for Him,
Grow near and nearer Him with all delight;
But then we shall not any more be called
To suffer, which is our appointment here.
Canst thou not suffer then one hour,—or two?

The poem ends with lines for those who cannot feel His presence or see His face. This darkness is the one last trial.

Christ was forsaken, so must thou be too.
Thou wilt not see the face nor feel the hand.
Only the cruel crushing of the feet,
When through the bitter night the Lord comes down

To tread the winepress.—Not by sight, but faith,
Endure, endure,—be faithful to the end!

Jesus' word "remain" or "abide" (in Him, in His love), repeated
ten times in John 15, means being at home in Him, living constantly in His presence and in harmony with His will. It does not
at all mean unmitigated suffering (the vine isn't cut back every
day!). For those of us who are not at the moment in pain, may we
not let slip any cross Jesus may present to us, any little way of let-
ting go of ourselves, any smallest task to do with gladness and
humility, any disappointment accepted with grace and silence.
These are His appointments. If we miss them here, we'll not find
them again in this world or in any other.

∽∽∽

The Incarnation Is A Thing Too Wonderful

Some things are simply too wonderful for explanation—the navigational system of the Arctic tern, for example. How does it find its way over twelve thousand miles of ocean from its nesting grounds in the Arctic to its wintering grounds in the Antarctic! Ornithologists have conducted all sorts of tests without finding the answer. *Instinct* is the best they can offer—no explanation at all, merely a way of saying that they really have no idea. A Laysan albatross was once released 3,200 miles from its nest in the Midway Islands. It was back home in ten days.

The migration of birds is a thing too wonderful.

When the angel Gabriel told Mary, "You will be with child and give birth to a son," she had a simple question about the natural: How can this be, since I am a virgin?!

The answer had to do not with the natural but with something far more mysterious than the tern's navigation—something, in fact, entirely supernatural: "The Holy Spirit will come upon you, and the Most High will overshadow you" (Luke 1:35, NIV). That was too wonderful, and Mary was silent. She had no question about the supernatural. She was satisfied with God's answer.

The truth about the Incarnation is a thing too wonderful for us. Who can fathom what really took place first in a virgin's womb in Nazareth and then in a stable in Bethlehem!

At the end of the book of Job, instead of answering his questions, God revealed to Job the mystery of Who He was. Then Job despised himself. "I have uttered what I did not understand,/ things too *wonderful* for me, which I did not know" (Job 42:3, RSV).

In one of David's "songs of ascents" he wrote, "My heart is not proud, O Lord,/ my eyes are not haughty;/ I do not concern myself with great matters/ or things *too wonderful* for me./ But I have stilled and quieted my soul; / like a weaned child with its mother,/ like a weaned child is my soul within me" (Psalm 131:1,2, NIV).

A close and fretful inquiry into how spiritual things "work" is an exercise in futility. Even wondering how "natural" things are going to work if you bring God into them—how God will answer a prayer for money, for example, or how your son-in-law is going to find a house for eight in southern California (on a pastor's salary)— is sometimes an awful waste of energy. God *knows how.* Why should I bother my head about it if I've turned it over to Him? If the Word of the Lord to us is that we are "predestined according to the plan of him who works out everything in conformity with his purpose" (Ephesians 1:11, NIV), we may apprehend this fact by faith alone. By believing that God means just what He says, and by acting upon the word (faith always requires action), we apprehend it—we take hold of it, we make it our own. We cannot make it our own by mere reason—"I don't see how such-and-such an incident can possibly have anything to do with any divine 'plan.'"

Why should we *see* how! Is it not sufficient that we are told that it is so? We need not see. We need only believe and proceed on the basis of that assured fact.

Mary's acceptance of the angel's answer to her innocent question was immediate, though she could not imagine the intricacies and mysteries of its working in her young virgin body. She surrendered herself utterly to God in trust and obedience.

Do you *understand* what is going on in the invisible realm of your life with God? Do you *see* how the visible things relate to the hidden Plan and Purpose? Probably not. As my second husband Addison Leitch used to say, "You can't unscrew the Inscrutable." But you do see at least one thing, maybe a very little thing, that He wants you to do. "Now what I am commanding you today is not too difficult [other translations say too hard, too wonderful] for you or beyond your reach. It is not up in heaven.... nor is it beyond the sea.... no, the word is very near you; it is in your mouth and in your heart so you may obey it" (Deuteronomy 30:11-14, NIV).

Let it suffice you, as it sufficed Mary, to know that God knows. If it's time to work, get on with your job. If it's time to go to bed, go to sleep in peace. Let the Lord of the Universe do the worrying.

The Supremacy of Christ

L ast October I received a copy of the Auca (now known as Waorani) translation of the New Testament. The orthography has been greatly altered since my day, so I can't read much of it now, but leafing through the pages I thought long, long thoughts. I had had nothing to do with the translation. I was with the Aucas only two years, during which Rachel Saint and I worked on reducing the language to writing, but we had barely begun to translate a few Bible stories when my daughter Valerie and I returned to Quichua work.

Sometimes I am asked to speak to young people who are toying with the idea of being missionaries. They want to know how I discovered the will of God. The first thing was to settle once and for all the supremacy of Christ in my life, I tell them. I put myself utterly and forever at His disposal, which means turning over *all* the rights: to myself, my body, my self-image, my notions of how I am to serve my Master. Oswald Chambers calls it "breaking the husk of my individual independence of God." Until that break comes, all the rest is "pious fraud." I tell these earnest kids that the will of God is always *different* from what they expect, always *bigger*, and, ultimately, infinitely more *glorious* than their wildest imaginings.

But there will be deaths to die. Paul found that out—daily, he said. That is the price of following the way of the cross—of course. If our object is to save others we must be clear that we cannot save ourselves. Jesus couldn't either.

This scares people. Yet what is there to fear when Christ holds first place in our lives? Where, other than in the will of the Father, shall we expect to find significance, security, and serenity?

God's guidance for me has been so different from my early notions—*I* was to be a jungle missionary for life! The complete futility, *humanly* speaking, of all the language work I did (Colorado, Quichua, and Auca, for various reasons, all came to nothing) was a deep lesson in the supremacy of Christ. Whom had I set out to serve? May He not do as He wills, then, with His servant and with that servant's work? Is anything offered to Christ ever wasted? I thought about the sacrifices of Old Testament times. When a man brought a lamb, the priest laid it on the altar, slit its throat, and burned it. The offering, then, was *accepted*. But what was left of it? Amy Carmichael, Irish missionary to India and author of forty books, taught me the implications of a *living sacrifice*. She wrote:

"But these strange ashes, Lord, this nothingness,
This baffling sense of loss?"
Son, was the anguish of my stripping less
Upon the torturing cross?
Was I not brought into the dust of death,
A worm, and no man, I;
Yea, turned to ashes by the vehement breath
Of fire, on Calvary?
O son beloved, *this* is thy heart's desire:
This, and no other thing
Follows the fall of the Consuming Fire
On the burnt offering.
Go on and taste the joy set high, afar,—
No joy like that to thee;
See how it lights the way like some great star.
Come now, and follow me.

I want to put it down right here that I have certainly "tasted the joy." I cannot imagine a more wonderfully blessed life than mine. Faithfulness of a loving Father—that's what I've found, every day of every week of every year, and it gets better. How I do hope those prospective missionaries will believe me!

Lord of All Seasons

A few years ago I spoke to a group of women in Florida about Jesus Christ being "Lord of All Seasons." The topic was their choice, and I found myself, as usual, tested along the very lines on which I was going to speak. During the previous week, Lars and I had learned that all twenty-eight of the nice new (and very expensive) windows we had installed in our new house *leaked*. I was anxious about many things—my mother's health, my coming grandchild, a new word processor which I wasn't sure I was smart enough to learn to use, and (alas!) a tooth which seemed about to fall out. What a list of varied things to worry about.

But Jesus died for me! He's risen and coming again! He has given me an inheritance that nothing can "destroy or spoil or wither" (1 Peter 1:4, NEB) and a Kingdom which is unshakable (Hebrews 12:28). That's the gospel. Has it anything to do with leaking windows, computers, grandchildren, teeth? Well, I told myself, if it hasn't, you've got no business getting up in front of those women and opening your mouth at all. If I can't give thanks, trust, and worship the Lord in every "season," in the face of any set of facts which may touch my life, I am not really a believer. It is here, in my corner of God's earth, that I am assigned my lessons in the School of Faith.

P.S. Later: They fixed the windows for us, but then we found that all four of the outside doors needed to be fixed. God hadn't finished with us yet.

∽∾∽

The Ultimate Contradiction

Two people were walking along a stony road long ago. They were deep in conversation about everything that had happened. Things could not have been worse, it seemed, and I suppose the road was longer and dustier and stonier than it had ever been to them, though they had traveled it many times. As they trudged along, trying to make sense out of the scuttling of their hopes, a stranger joined them and wanted to know what they were talking about.

"You must be the only stranger in Jerusalem who hasn't heard all the things that have happened there recently!" said one of the two, whose name was Cleopas.

It seemed that the stranger had no idea what things he referred to, so Cleopas explained that there was a man from the village of Nazareth, Jesus by name, who was clearly a prophet, but He had been executed by crucifixion a few days before.

"We were hoping He was the one who was to come and set Israel free."

Things had been bad for Israel for a long time, and those who understood the ancient writings looked for a liberator and a savior. Cleopas and his companion had pinned their hopes on this Nazarene—surely He was the one God had sent, a prophet "strong in what he did and what he said" (Luke 24:19 PHILLIPS). But those hopes had been completely crushed. He had been killed and even His body could not be found. Where were they to turn now?

The story goes on to tell how the stranger explained to them that they had not really understood what the prophets had written, and that this death which had so shattered their faith was inevitable if the Messiah was to "find his glory."

But what a strange phrase—"find his glory." What could it mean? I can imagine the two looking at each other in bewilderment. This shameful death—in order to find his *glory?*

When they reached their destination the stranger was about to go further but they persuaded him to stay with them. As they sat down to eat he picked up the loaf of bread, gave thanks, broke it, and gave it to them. Suddenly they recognized him. *Jesus!* The two who sat with Him had not been pessimists. They had indeed had hopes. But what puny hopes theirs had been. In their wildest optimism they could not have dreamed of the glory they now saw. A resurrection, the ultimate contradiction to all of the world's woes, had taken place. They saw Jesus with their own eyes. What must their own words have seemed to them if they thought about what they had said: "We were hoping..."? They could not deny that those hopes had died, but what insane dreamer could have imagined the possibility that had become a reality here at their own supper table? Their savior had come back. He had walked with them. He was in their house. He was eating the very bread they had provided.

If resurrection is a fact—and there would be no Easter if it were not—then there is no situation so hopeless, no horizon so black, that God cannot there "find His glory." The truth is that without those ruined hopes, without that death, without the suffering that He called inevitable, the glory itself would be impossible. Why the universe is so arranged we must leave to the One who arranged it, but that it is so we are bound to believe.

And when we find ourselves most hopeless, the road most taxing, we may also find that it is then that the Risen Christ catches up to us on the way, better than our dreams, beyond all our hopes. For it is He—not His gifts, not His power, not what He can do for us, but He Himself—who comes and makes Himself known to us. And this is the one pure joy for those who sorrow.

And yet... and yet we sorrow. The glorious fact of the resurrection is the very heart of our faith. We believe it. We bank all our hopes on it. And yet we sorrow. It is still appointed unto man once to die, and those who are left must grieve—not as those without hope, for the beloved will be resurrected. The "ultimate contradiction," however, seems very far in the future. There is no incongruity in the human tears and the pure joy of the presence of Christ, for He wept human tears too.

When we learned recently from dear friends that they had lost their baby, this is what I wrote to them (I've been asked to print it here for others who are bereaved):

"Your little note was waiting for us when we returned yesterday from Canada. How our hearts went running to you, weeping with you, wishing we could see your faces and tell you our sympathies. Yet it is 'no strange thing' that has happened to you, as Peter said in his epistle (1 Peter 4:12)—it gives you a share in Christ's suffering. To me this is one of the deepest but most comforting of all the mysteries of suffering. Not only does He enter into grief in the fullest understanding, suffer with us and for us, but in the very depths of sorrow He allows us, in His mercy, to enter into *His*; gives us a share, permits us the high privilege of 'filling up' that which is lacking (Colossians 1:24) in His own. He makes, in other words, something redemptive out of our broken hearts, if those hearts are offered up to Him. We are told that He will never despise a broken heart. It is an acceptable sacrifice when offered wholly to Him for His transfiguration. Oh, there is so *much* for us to learn here, but it will not be learned in a day or a week. Level after level must be plumbed as we walk with the Shepherd, and He will do His purifying, purging, forging, shaping work in us, that we may be shaped to the image of Christ Himself. Such shaping takes a hammer, a chisel, and a file—painful tools, a painful process.

"Your dear tiny Laura is in the Shepherd's arms. She will never have to suffer. She knew only the heaven of the womb (the safest place in all the world—apart from the practice of abortion) and now she knows the perfect heaven of God's presence. I'm sure that your prayer for both your children has been that God would fulfill

His purpose in them. It is the highest and best we can ask for our beloved children. He has already answered that prayer for Laura.

"Do you know the *Letters of Samuel Rutherford* (1600-1661)? He wrote so beautifully to mothers who had lost children. Here is one:

> Grace rooteth not out the affections of a mother, but putteth them on His wheel who maketh all things new, that they may be refined; therefore sorrow for a dead child is allowed to you, though by measure and ounceweights; the redeemed of the Lord have not a dominion or lordship over their sorrow and other affections, to lavish out Christ's goods at their pleasure.... He commandeth you to weep; and that princely One took up to heaven with Him a man's heart to be a compassionate High Priest. The cup ye drink was at the lip of sweet Jesus, and He drank of it.... Ye are not to think it a bad bargain for your beloved daughter that she died—she hath gold for copper and brass, eternity for time. All the knot must be that she died too soon, too young, in the morning of her life; but sovereignty must silence your thoughts. I was in your condition: I had but two children, and both are dead since I came hither. The supreme and absolute Former of all things giveth not an account of any of His matters. The good Husbandman may pluck His roses and gather His lilies at midsummer, and, for ought I dare say, in the beginning of the first summer month; and he may transplant young trees out of the lower ground to the higher, where they may have more of the sun and a more free air, at any season of the year. The goods are His own. The Creator of time and winds did a merciful injury (if I may borrow the word) to nature in landing the passenger so early.

"Jesus learned obedience by the things which He *suffered*, not by the things which He enjoyed. In order to fit you both for His purposes both here and in eternity, He has lent you this sorrow. But He bears the heavier end of the Cross laid upon you! Be sure that Lars and I are praying for you, dear friends."

Section Two

God's Curriculum

O Lord our governor, we beseech Thee, of Thy mercy,
That we may have the heavenly vision,
And behold things as they seem unto Thee,
That the turmoil of this world may be seen by us
To be bringing forth the sweet peace of the eternal years,
And that in all the troubles and sorrows or our own hearts
We may behold good, and so, with quiet mind
And inward peace, careless of outward storm,
We may do the duty of life which brings to us
A quiet heart, ever trusting in Thee.

We give Thee thanks for all Thy mercy.
We beseech Thy forgiveness of all our sins.
We pray Thy guidance in all things,
Thy presence in the hour of death,
Thy glory in the life to come.
Of Thy mercy hear us,
Through Jesus Christ our Lord.
Amen.

George Dawson, 1821-1876

CRCRCR

God's Curriculum

One day recently something lit a fuse of anger in someone who then burned me with hot words. I felt sure I didn't deserve this response, but when I ran to God about it, He reminded me of part of a prayer I'd been using lately: "Teach me to treat all that comes to me with peace of soul and with firm conviction that Your will governs all."

Where could that kind of peace come from? Only from God, who gives "not as the world gives."

His will that I should be burned? Here we must tread softly. His will *governs* all. In a wrong-filled world we suffer (and cause) many a wrong. God is there to heal and comfort and forgive. He who brought blessing to many out of the sin of the jealous brothers against Joseph means this hurt for my ultimate blessing and, I think, for an increase of love between me and the one who hurt me. Love is very patient, very kind. Love never seeks its own. Love looks to God for his grace to help.

"It was not you who sent me here but God," Joseph said to his brothers. "You meant to do me harm; but God meant to bring good out of it" (Genesis 45:8, 50:20, NEB).

There is a philosophy of secular education which holds that the student ought to be allowed to assemble his own curriculum according to his preferences. Few students have a strong basis for making these choices, not knowing how little they know. Ideas of what they need to learn are not only greatly limited but greatly distorted. What they need is *help*—from those who know more than they do.

Mercifully, God does not leave us to choose our own curriculum. His wisdom is perfect, His knowledge embraces not only all worlds but the individual hearts and minds of each of His loved children. With intimate understanding of our deepest needs and individual capacities, He chooses our curriculum. We need only ask, "Give us this day our daily bread, our daily lessons, our homework." An angry retort from someone may be just the occasion we need in which to learn not only longsuffering and forgiveness, but meekness and gentleness; fruits not *born* in us but borne only by the Spirit. As Amy Carmichael wrote, "A cup brimful of sweetness cannot spill even one drop of bitter water, no matter how suddenly jarred" (From her book *If* published by Christian Literature Crusade).

God's curriculum for all who sincerely want to know Him and do His will will always include lessons we wish we could skip. But the more we apply ourselves, the more honestly we can say what the psalmist said: "I, thy servant, will study thy statutes. / Thy instruction is my continual delight; / I turn to it for counsel. / I will run the course set out in thy commandments, / for they gladden my heart" (Psalm 119:23, 24, 32, NEB).

⌒⌒⌒

Little Things

When we were growing up our parents taught us, by both word and example, to pay attention to little things. If you do a thing at all, do it thoroughly: make the sheets really *smooth* on the bed, sweep all the corners and move all the chairs when you sweep the kitchen, roll the toothpaste tube neatly and put the cap back on, clean the hair out of your brush each time you use it, hang your towel straight on the rod, fold your napkin and put it into the silver ring before you leave the table, never wet your finger when you turn pages. They kept promises made to us as faithfully as they kept those made to adults. They taught us to do the same. You didn't accept an invitation to a party and then not turn up, or agree to help with the Vacation Bible School and back out because a more interesting activity presented itself. The only financial debt my parents ever incurred was a mortgage on a house, which my father explained was in a special class because it was *real* estate which would always have value.

When I went to boarding school the same principles I had been taught at home were emphasized. There was a hallway with small oriental rugs which we called "Character Hall" because the head-mistress, Mrs. DuBose, could look down that hall from the arm-chair where she sat in the lobby and spot any student who kicked up the corner of a rug and did not replace it. She would call out to correct him, "It's those tiny little things in your life which will crack you up when you get out of this school!" In the *little* things our character was revealed. Our response would make or break us. "Don't go around with a Bible under your arm if you didn't sweep under the bed," she said, for she would have no pious talk coming out of a messy room.

"Great thoughts go best with common duties. Whatever therefore may be your office regard it as a fragment in an immeasurable ministry of love" (Bishop Brooke Foss Westcott, b. 1825).

It is not easy to find children or adults who are dependable, careful, thorough, and faithful. So many lives seem honeycombed with small failures, neglectful of the little things that make the difference between order and chaos. Perhaps it is because they are so seldom taught that visible things are signs of an invisible reality; that common duties may be "an immeasurable ministry of love." The spiritual training of souls must be inseparable from practical disciplines, as Jesus so plainly taught; "The man who can be trusted in little things can be trusted in great; the man who is dishonest in little things will be dishonest in great. If then you cannot be trusted with money, that tainted thing, who will trust you with genuine riches! And if you cannot be trusted with what is not yours, who will give you what is your very own?" (Luke 16:10-12, JB). (The footnote to "your very own" says, "Jesus is speaking of the most intimate possessions a man can have; these are spiritual.")

CRECD

What Do You Mean by Submission?

People are always asking me this. What *is* this business of "submission" you're always talking about? We're not really very comfortable with this. Seems kinds of negative. Sounds as though women are not worth as much as men. Aren't women supposed to exercise their gifts? Can't they ever open their mouths?

I wouldn't be very comfortable with that kind of submission either. As a matter of fact, I'm not particularly comfortable with any kind, but since it was God's idea and not mine, I had better come to terms with what the Bible says about it and stop rejecting the whole thing just because it is so often misunderstood and wrongly defined. I came across a lucid example of what it means in 1 Chronicles 11:10, NEB: "Of David's heroes these were the chief, men who lent their full strength to his government and, with all Israel, joined in making him king." There it is. The recognition, first of all, of God-given authority. Recognizing it, accepting it, they then lent their full strength to it, and did everything in their power to make him—not them—*king*.

Christians—both men and women—recognize first the authority of Christ. They pray "Thy will be done." They set about making an honest effort to cooperate with what He is doing, straightening out the kinks in their own lives according to His wishes. A Christian woman, then, in submission to *God*, recognizes the divinely assigned authority of her husband (he didn't earn it, remember, he received it by appointment). She then sets about lending her full strength to helping him do what he's supposed to do, be what he's supposed to be—her *head*. She's not always trying to get her own way. She's trying to make it easier for him to do his job. She seeks to contribute to *his* purpose, not to scheme how to accomplish her own.

If this sounds suspiciously like some worn-out traditionalist view, or (worse) like a typical Elisabeth Elliot opinion, test it with the straightedge of Scripture. What does submission to Christ mean? "Wives, submit yourselve to your husbands, *as to the Lord.*" Compare and connect.

CROCO

Where Will Complaining Get You?

When we were in Dallas for a visit, we were the guests of our dear friend Nina Jean Obel. As we sat one morning in her beautiful sunshiny yellow and pale-green kitchen, she reminded us of how, in the story in Deuteronomy 1, when the Israelites were within fourteen days of the Promised Land, they complained. Complaining was a habit which had angered Moses, their leader, to the point where he wished he were dead. "How can I bear unaided the heavy burden you are to me, and put up with your complaints?" he asked. They headed for Horeb, but when they reached the hill country of the Amorites they refused to believe the promises and insisted on sending spies to see what sort of a land it was. The spies came back with a glowing report, but the people didn't believe that either. Never mind the lovely fruit the land offered. There were giants in the land; they'd all be killed. There were huge fortifications towering to the sky. How would they ever conquer them?

It was the neurotic's attitude. No answer would do. No solution offered was good enough. The promises of God, the direction of Moses, the report of the spies—all unacceptable. The people had already made up their minds that they didn't like anything God was doing. They "muttered treason." They said the Lord hated them. He brought them out only to have them wiped out by the Amorites. O God, what a fate. O God, why do you treat us this way? O God, how are we going to get out of this? It's your fault. You hate us. Moses hates us. Everything and everybody's against us.

Nina Jean said she made up her mind that if complaining was the reason God's people were denied the privilege of entering Canaan, she was going to quit it. She set herself a tough task: absolutely no complaining for fourteen days. It was a revelation to her—first, of how strong a habit it had become, and second, of how different the whole world looked when she did not complain. I get the impression when I'm around Nina Jean that the fourteen-day trial was enough to kick the habit. I've never heard her complain.

It's not just the sunshine and the colors that make her kitchen a nice place to be. It's that Nina Jean is there. I'd like to create that sort of climate for the people I'm around. I've set myself the same task.

~~~

Humdudgeons or Contentment

The word *humdudgeon* is a new one to me and I like the sound of it. It means "a loud complaint about a trifle." Heard any of those lately around your house? One mother thought of an excellent antidote: all humdudgeons must be presented not orally but in writing, "of two hundred words or more." There was a sudden marked reduction in whining and complaining.

Parents, by example, teach their children to whine. No wonder it is so difficult to teach them not to! Listen to conversations in the elevator, at the hairdresser's, at the next table in the restaurant. Everybody's whining about everything—weather, health, the president, the IRS, the insurance mess, traffic, the kids.

Human life is full of trouble, which doesn't come from the dust, said Job's friend Eliphaz, nor does it sprout from the ground. Man is *born* to trouble. Compare your list of troubles with one famous man's:

1. He had a difficult childhood
2. Less than one year of formal schooling
3. Failed in business at age 31
4. Defeated for legislature at 32
5. Failed again in business at 33
6. Elected to the legislature at 34
7. His fiancée died when he was 35
8. Defeated for speaker at 38

9. Defeated for electorate at 40
10. At 42 married a woman who became a burden, not a help
11. Only one of four sons lived past age 18
12. Defeated for congress at 43
13. Elected to congress at 46
14. Defeated for congress at 48
15. Defeated for senate at 55
16. Defeated for vice president at 56
17. Defeated for senate at 58
18. Finally elected president.

He was Abraham Lincoln, of course. When I look at his list of setbacks, I wonder if I've ever had a problem.

Adler said, "It is a categorical demand of the neurotic's lifespan that he should fail through the guilt of others and thus be free of responsibility." That sobered me. Is my response to failure instantly to lay the blame on somebody else? Is there always an excuse, a complaint, an inner whine!

A spirit of calm contentment always accompanies true godliness. The deep peace that comes from deep trust in God's lovingkindness is not destroyed even by the worst of circumstances, for those Everlasting Arms are still cradling us, we are always "under the Mercy." Corrie ten Boom was "born to trouble" like the rest of us, but in a German concentration camp she jumped to her feet every morning and exuberantly sang "Stand Up, Stand Up for Jesus!" She thanked the Lord for the little parade of ants that marched through her cell, bringing her company. When Paul and Silas were in prison, they prayed and sang. It isn't troubles that make saints, but their response to troubles. Even miracles can't make us holy. Paul reminded the Corinthians that the Israelites were *all* guided by the same cloud, *all* had the experience of passing through the sea, *all* ate the same supernatural food, and *all* drank the same supernatural drink. "In spite of this, most of them failed to please God and their corpses littered the desert" (1 Corinthians 10:5, JB). The reason for His displeasure came down to a single root: discontent, which included "wicked lusts for forbidden things" (idols and illicit sex, for which 23,000 were killed in one day) and *complaining* because they wanted things perfectly legitimate in themselves which God had not given—leeks and onions and garlic and cucumbers and fish—and stood at their tent doors, parents and children together wailing: "Here we are, wasting away, stripped of everything; there is nothing but manna for us to look at!" (Numbers 11:6, JB). Many were struck with a plague and died.

When Paul's flesh was tormented by a sharp thorn, he naturally wanted it removed. He made this request known to God, but the answer was No. God didn't change Paul's physical condition, He changed his spiritual one. He gave him what he needed more than healing. He gave him the high ministry of heaven called grace. Paul not only accepted the answer, he learned even to be very thankful for weakness itself, for "power comes to its full strength in weakness."

Everything about which we are tempted to complain may be the very instrument whereby the Potter intends to shape His clay into the image of His Son—a headache, an insult, a long line at the check-out, someone's rudeness or failure to say thank you, misunderstanding, disappointment, interruption. As Amy Carmichael said, "See in it a chance to die," meaning a chance to leave self behind and say YES to the will of God, to be "conformable unto His death." Not a morbid martyr-complex but a peaceful and happy contentment in the assurance that goodness and mercy follow us all the days of our lives. Wouldn't our children learn godliness if they saw the example of contentment instead of complaint? acceptance instead of rebellion? peace instead of frustration?

May ours be the spirit of the seventeen-year-old Lady Jane Grey, who prayed this prayer in her prison cell before she was beheaded in 1554:

O merciful God, be Thou unto me
A strong Tower of defence,
I humbly entreat Thee.
Give me grace to await thy leisure,
And patiently to bear
What Thou doest unto me;
Nothing doubting or mistrusting

Thy goodness towards me;
For Thou knowest what is good for me
Better than I do.
Therefore do with me in all things
What Thou wilt;
Only arm me, I beseech Thee,
With Thine armor,
That I may stand fast;
Above all things taking to me
The shield of faith;
Praying always that I may
Refer myself wholly to Thy will,
Abiding Thy pleasure, and comforting myself
In those troubles which it shall please Thee
To send me, seeing such troubles are
Profitable for me; and I am
Assuredly persuaded that all Thou doest
Cannot but be well; and unto Thee
Be all honor and glory. Amen.

ᗢᗢᗢ

Several Ways to Make Yourself Miserable

1. Count your troubles, name them one by one—at the breakfast table, if anybody will listen, or as soon as possible thereafter.
2. Worry every day about something. Don't let yourself get out of practice. It won't add a cubit to your stature but it might burn a few calories.
3. Pity yourself. If you do enough of this, nobody else will have to do it for you.
4. Devise clever but decent ways to serve God *and* mammon. After all, a man's gotta live.
5. Make it your business to find out what the Joneses are buying this year and where they're going. Try to do them at least one better even if you have to take out another loan to do it.
6. Stay away from absolutes. It's what's right for *you* that matters. Be your own person and don't allow yourself to get hung up on what others expect of you.
7. Make sure you get your rights. Never mind other people's. You have your life to live, they have theirs.
8. Don't fall into any compassion traps—the sort of situation where people can walk all over you. If you get too involved in other people's troubles, you may neglect your own.
9. Don't let Bible reading and prayer get in the way of what's really relevant—things like TV and newspapers. Invisible things are eternal. You want to stick with the visible ones—they're where it's at *now*.

∽∽∽

Indecision

It is painfully obvious that many young people today have an awful time making up their minds about anything. They're not "really sure" what college to go to, what to major in, whom to room with, what career to prepare for, whether or whom to marry, whether to bother with children if they do marry, when to bother with them, what to do with them if they get them, whether to attempt to instill any values in their children (not to make up your mind on this issue is, of course, already to have instilled a value in the mind of the child).

Garry Trudeau, author of the cartoon "Doonesbury," has noticed this prevalent indecisiveness. In one strip he has a young man appearing for an interview with the president of an advertising company.

"So you want to be an ad man, eh, son?" says the executive.

"Well, I think so, sir," says the youth. "I mean, I can't be certain, of course, but it seemed worth looking into, you know, to see if it worked out, if it felt right and... I... uh..."

I guess there's nothing new about indecision. James wrote about it in his epistle, and he shows that the remedy for it is trust. He tells us to ask for wisdom if we don't know what to do. "But when you ask him, be sure that you really expect him to tell you, for a doubtful mind will be as unsettled as a wave of the sea that is driven and tossed by the wind; and every decision you then make will be uncertain, as you turn first this way and then that. If you don't ask with faith, don't expect the Lord to give you any solid answer" (James 1:6-8, LB).

Father, let our faithful mind
Rest, on Thee alone inclined;
Every anxious thought repress,
Keep our souls in perfect peace.

C. Wesley

∽∾∿

The Fear of Man or Woman

"The majority of men have thought of women as sublime separately but horrible as a herd," noted the wise G.K. Chesterton. Alas. Are we so formidable? Robert Bly, in his best-selling *Iron John*, declares that men are petrified of female anger. Then there's a *Time* correspondent named Sam Allis who says "Women are often daunting obstacles to male peace of mind, and for all their brave talk, men remain utterly flummoxed by the situation."

"The fear of man bringeth a snare," according to God's Word. Meseemeth the fear of woman bringeth a worse one. These comments have set me thinking (again) about fear in general. If men and women were surer of their God there would be more genuine manliness, womanliness, and godliness in the world, and a whole lot less fear of each other.

Jesus told us not to fear those who can kill only the body, but rather to fear Him who can destroy both soul and body in hell—in other words, *fear God and fear nothing else*. Moses, by faith, "left Egypt, not fearing the king's anger; he persevered because he saw him who is invisible" (Hebrews 11:27, NIV). When Daniel learned of King Darius's decree forbidding prayer to any god or man except the king himself, he proceeded with his regular manner of worship, on his knees, windows open, "just as he had done before," and was caught in the act (Daniel 6). He feared God; therefore, he feared neither the king nor the lions. His three friends, Shadrach, Meshach, and Abednego, faced with the choice between two evils, worshipping a golden image or burning to a crisp in a furnace, made an instant decision (Daniel 3). Fear of God made worship of an idol unthinkable. Fear of the fire was, by comparison, *thinkable*. That's manliness.

Uzziah, who became king of Judah when he was sixteen, was *taught* by Zechariah to fear God. A child who is not taught to fear wrongdoing when he is small will have great difficulty learning to fear God when he is a man. "Freedom from fear" is what Russell Kirk calls "a silly piece of demagogic sophistry," for we all have "a natural yearning for the challenge of the dreadful."

One of the nicest things any of the listeners to my broadcast, *Gateway to Joy*, has written to me came from a little girl: "You make me brave." Sometimes I wonder what has happened to words like courage and endurance. What reason is there in our feel-comfortable society ever to be brave? Very little, and, when you think about it, we miss it, don't we? To be really brave is to lay oneself open to charges of hypocrisy, of being "in denial," or out of touch with one's feelings. Moses charged Joshua to be strong and very courageous. Courage is not the absence of fear but the willingness to do the thing we fear. Go straight into the furnace or the lion's den. Were those men out of touch with their feelings or with reality? No. Nor was the psalmist who said, "When I *am* afraid, I *will* trust" (Psalm 56:3, NIV). There's a big difference between feeling and willing.

In George MacDonald's *Sir Gibbie* the boy (Gibbie) is up in the mountains in a storm. He hears the sound of the river in flood and realizes it is headed straight for the cottage. He shoots after it. "He is not terrified. One believing like him in the perfect Love and perfect Will of a Father of men, as the fact of facts, fears nothing. Fear is faithlessness.... A perfect faith would lift us absolutely above fear. It is in the cracks, crannies, and gulfy faults of our belief, the gaps that are not faith, that the snow of apprehension settles and the ice of unkindness forms."

Do you feel, in spite of all the promises of God, as helpless as a worm today? There's a special word for you too: "Do not fear; I will help you. Do not be afraid, O worm Jacob, O little Israel, for I myself will help you" (Isaiah 41:14, NIV).

Spiritual Opposition

When Lars and I returned from a fortnight in Scotland and England there was the expected pile-up of work awaiting us, and the usual temptation to feel overwhelmed by it. The suitcase had to be unpacked, clothes washed, mail opened, read, and answered. The house had been partially cleaned by the student who lives with us, but upstairs I had to deal with the dust. There were phone messages waiting, and phone calls we needed to make to family members. Do you know the feeling of utter inadequacy to cope? I'm sure you do. But I believe the enemy of our souls is specially alert at such times, seeking to use them to turn us in on ourselves rather than upwards to the One who stands ready to be our Refuge and Helper.

Laying all the work before the Lord on the first morning after our return, I asked for His help to do it faithfully, carefully, and in an orderly way. I believe He answered that prayer—I'm sure He did. Everything that had to be done in those first three days was done, and I couldn't possibly have done it on my own. Then there was the lovely respite of Sunday, with time to read and think. I looked forward to tackling Monday's work (radio talks, scheduling of speaking) at a clean desk.

Monday came. The day was committed to God as always. But I felt like the wheels of the Egyptian chariots which "drave heavily." There were interruptions, distractions. I could not get on as expected. My mind was dull, confused. At the end of the day I could not see what I had done with my time.

Tuesday was a continuation of the day before. Where had those hours gone? I took my usual walk after lunch around Ocean Drive—a cloudless sky, a glittering sea. I walked alone, talking to

God about my failures, asking Him to clarify things. When I got back home, such an unexpected source of help came to hand—a letter written to my father thirty years ago by an old missionary. Things were not going well at that time with the paper, *The Sunday School Times*, of which my father was editor, and he was on the verge of what was then called a nervous breakdown. He had asked counsel of this old veteran, E.L. Langston, in Africa.

"The devil does not like that paper nor its articles, and is evidently attacking you in your inmost heart, not causing you to doubt so much as causing a spirit of discontent. Fortunately we both know that temptation is not sin, it is yielding to temptation that causes us to sin and I feel that you must count it joy that you are passing through these times of difficulty, for they are sure signs that the Lord is blessing you....

"There is another reason, I think, for the cause of the feeling within us. It comes from the flesh and self-introspection. It is good for us to look at self and know how loathsome it is, but with one look at self we must take ten looks at Christ....

"No one goes to church more than the devil does, and no one appears as an angel of light as he does. We are in the thick of facing powers of darkness who are determined to rob us of Him and rob God of us, and you and I, my brother, have just got to hope in Christ and rely on Him for His Spirit to direct our thoughts, our ways, and our works so that it is not us but Christ in us."

Wasn't it wonderful that that letter had been preserved so that I "chanced upon it" in the hour of my need? But that is so like the Lord, for it is through the tender austerity of our very troubles that the Son of Man comes knocking. In every event He seeks an entrance to my heart, yes, even in my most helpless, futile, fruitless moments. The very cracks and empty crannies of my life, my perplexities and hurts and botched-up jobs, He wants to fill with Himself, His joy, His life. The more unsatisfactory my "performance," the more He calls me to share His yoke. I should know by now that mine makes me tired and overburdened. He urges me to learn of Him: "I am gentle and humble in heart."

∞∞

The Gift of Work

The principal cause of boredom is the hatred of work. People are trained from childhood to hate it. Parents often feel guilty about making children do anything but the merest gestures toward work. Perhaps the children are required to make their beds and, in a feeble and half-hearted fashion, tidy up their rooms once a month or so. But take full responsibility to clear the table, load the dishwasher, scrub the pots, wipe the counters? How many have the courage to ask this of a ten-year-old? It would be too much to ask of many ten-year-olds because parents have seriously asked nothing of them when they were two or three. Children quickly pick up the parents' negative attitudes toward work and think of it as something most sedulously to be avoided.

Our Lord and Savior worked. There is little doubt that He served in the carpenter shop under the instruction of His earthly father Joseph, putting in long hours, learning skill, care, responsibility, and above all, the glory of work as a gift to glorify His heavenly Father. He did always those things that please the Father. Later he chose almost all His disciples from those who labored with their hands. Even the apostle Paul, a man of brilliant intellect, made tents.

Booker T. Washington, an African-American who grew up in the South when members of his race were expected to do the hardest and dirtiest jobs, learned his greatest lesson from the example of a Christian woman. A New Englander, the founder of the Hampton Institute, she herself washed the windows the day before school started, so it would be nice for those children who had been born slaves.

Is work a necessary evil, even a curse? A Christian who spent many years in Soviet work camps, learning to know work at its most brutal, its most degrading and dehumanizing, testified that he took pride in it, did the best he could, worked to the limit of his strength each day. Why? Because he saw it as a gift from God, coming to him from the hand of God, the very will of God for him. He remembered that Jesus did not make benches and roofbeams and plow handles by means of miracles, but by means of saw, axe, and adze.

Wouldn't it make an astounding difference, not only in the quality of the work we do (in office, schoolroom, factory, kitchen, or backyard), but also in our satisfaction, even our joy, if we recognized God's gracious gift in every single task, from making a bed or bathing a baby to drawing a blueprint or selling a computer? If our children saw us doing "heartily as unto the Lord" all the work we do, they would learn true happiness. Instead of feeling that they must be allowed to do what they like, they would learn to like what they do.

St. Ignatius Loyola prayed, "Teach us, Good Lord, to labor and to ask for no reward save that of knowing that we do Thy will." As I learn to pray that prayer, I find that there are many more rewards that come along as fringe benefits. As we make an offering of our work, we find the truth of a principle Jesus taught: Fulfillment is not a goal to achieve, but always the by-product of sacrifice.

The Universal Thump

It's so refreshing to find some encouragement to work and to be cheerful and take orders, instead of what is more common today, an outright dislike, even hatred, of work and an unwillingness to take orders from anybody. We've really had just about enough of that, don't you think? So here's an antidote in the musings of a sailor in Herman Melville's great classic, *Moby Dick*:

> What of it if some old hunk of a sea-captain orders me to get a broom and sweep down the decks? What does that indignity amount to, weigh, I mean, in the scales of the New Testament? Do you think the archangel Gabriel thinks anything the less of me because I promptly and respectfully obey that old hunk in that particular instance? Who ain't a slave? Tell me that. Well, then, however the old sea-captains may order me about, I have the satisfaction of knowing that it is all right; that everybody else is one way or other served in much the same way—either in a physical or metaphysical point of view, that is; and so the universal thump is passed round, and all hands should rub each other's shoulder-blades, and be content.

Most of us are not exactly under the orders of "some old hunk of a sea-captain," but we *are* meant to be willing and cheerful servants of anybody who happens to need us. Have I a true servant-heart? I should have. I will not be anything like my Lord Jesus if I haven't, for He came not to be served but to serve. He set for us a radiant example of how practically He meant it. He washed feet. Knowing

Knowing His own origin and destiny, He did it with grace and He did it with love.

And what is our origin? Our destiny? We, too, "come from God and are going back to God." Is there any job, then, that is really "beneath us?" Any "thump" that we really mind?

"You, my brothers, were called to be free. But do not use your freedom to indulge the sinful nature; rather, serve one another in love" (Galatians 5:13, NIV).

Last summer a certain fifteen-year-old worked at a ranch, where his job included not only dishwashing but cleaning out the garbage truck. They weren't jobs he'd have opted for (he'd far rather have exercised horses or even mucked out stables), so I gave him "Whatever you do, work at it with all your heart, as working for the Lord, not for men, since you know that you will receive an inheritance from the Lord as a reward. *It is the Lord Christ you are serving*" (Colossians 3:23-24, NIV). He wrote me a sweet letter, said God was helping him.

∽∽∽

But I Have a
Graduate Degree

A woman was asked to speak to the women students of a seminary about job opportunities for those with seminary degrees. She writes, "I talked to them first principally about being, doing, and going as God wills (not who am I, but *whose* am I). Then I listed both traditional and creative ways to fulfill needs in the Kingdom of God. Three feminists were offended especially that I should mention a nanny among the 70+ jobs. But Aristotle was a 'nanny' to Alexander the Great! These women had bought into the values of the world and were ready to fight for their ten years of executive computer programming. They said my talk had 'put them down more than any man's.'"

Theology means the study of God, but if an earned degree in that field confers a position in life which makes servanthood "beneath us" (three women felt "put down"), something is badly amiss. "The servant is not greater than his master," Jesus said. "Once you have realized these things, you will find your happiness in doing them" (John 13:16, 17, PHILLIPS).

Happiness—never mind the "status" of the job. The disciples had been occupied with petty rivalries and questions about greatness. Jesus, "with the full knowledge that the Father had put everything into His hands" (John 13:3, PHILLIPS), took into those hands the dusty, calloused feet of each of the twelve, washed them, and dried them with a towel. It was His happiness to do the will of His Father, but it was a shock to those rugged men. The washing of feet hadn't occurred to them as coming under that heading, I suppose, even though they had heard the principle before. I can imagine the bewilderment on their faces. Can't you just hear Peter's tone as he says, *"You,* Lord, washing *my* feet?" (v. 6, NEB).

Values get skewed so easily nowadays, don't they? *Time* (Nov. 7, 1988) carried the testimony of one man who, according to the world's measurement of success, had hit the top. He was playwright Eugene O'Neill, and if it's success that makes people happy he should have been the happiest of men. He sounded like the most miserable: "I'm fed to the teeth with the damned theatre.... The game isn't worth the candle. If I got any real spiritual satisfaction out of success in the theatre it might compensate. But I don't. Success is as flat, spiritually speaking, as failure. After the unprecedented critical acclaim to *Mourning Becomes Electra* I was in bed nearly a week, overcome by the profoundest gloom and nervous exhaustion."

Lay O'Neill's words alongside Jesus': "Once you have realized these things you will find your happiness in doing them." It's hard for us earthbound mortals to realize them. It's easy to be beguiled by temporal rewards, short-lived promises of fulfillment. The brighter the prospects the world offers, the more obscure become the principles of the Kingdom in which, as Janet Erskine Stuart said, "humility and service are the only expression and measure of greatness."

CRORD

The Key to
Supernatural Power

The world cannot fathom strength proceeding from weakness, gain proceeding from loss, or power from meekness. Christians apprehend these truths very slowly, if at all, for we are strongly influenced by secular thinking. Let's stop and concentrate on what Jesus meant when He said that the *meek* would inherit the earth. Do we understand what meekness truly is? Think first about what it isn't.

It is not a naturally phlegmatic temperament. I knew a woman who was so phlegmatic that nothing seemed to make much difference to her at all. While drying dishes for her one day in her kitchen I asked where I should put a serving platter.

"Oh, I don't know. Wherever *you* think would be a good place," was her answer. I wondered how she managed to *find* things if there wasn't a place for everything (and everything in its place).

Meekness is not indecision or laziness or feminine fragility or loose sentimentalism or indifference or affable neutrality.

Meekness is most emphatically not *weakness*. Do you remember who was the meekest man in the Old Testament? Moses! (See Numbers 12:3). My mental image of him is not of a feeble man. It is shaped by Michelangelo's sculpture and painting and by the biblical descriptions. Think of him murdering the Egyptian, smashing the tables of the commandments, grinding the golden calf to a powder, scattering it on the water and making the Israelites drink it. Nary a hint of weakness there, nor in David who wrote, "The meek will he guide in judgment" (Psalm 25:9, KJV), nor in Isaiah, who wrote, "The meek also shall increase their joy in the Lord" (Isaiah 29:19, KJV).

The Lord Jesus was the Lamb of God, and when we think of lambs we think of meekness (and perhaps weakness), but He was also the Lion of Judah, and He said, "I am *meek* and lowly in heart" (Matthew 11:29, KJV). He told us that we can find rest for our souls if we will come to Him, take His yoke, and learn. What we must learn is meekness. It doesn't come naturally to any of us.

Meekness is teachability. "The meek will he teach his way" (Psalm 25:9, KJV). It is the readiness to be shown, which includes the readiness to lay down my fixed notions, my objections and "what ifs" or "but what abouts," my certainties about the rightness of what I have always done or thought or said. It is the child's glad "Show me! Is *this* the way? Please help me." We won't make it into the kingdom without that childlikeness, that simple willingness to be taught and corrected and helped. "Receive with meekness the engrafted word, which is able to save your souls" (James 1:21, KJV). Meekness is an explicitly spiritual quality, a fruit of the Spirit, learned, not inherited. It shows in the kind of attention we pay to one another, the tone of voice we use, the facial expression.

One weekend I spoke in Atlanta on this subject, and the following weekend I was to speak on it again in Philadelphia. As very often happens, I was sorely tested on that very point in the few days in between. That sore test was my chance to be taught and changed and helped. At the same time I was strongly tempted to indulge in the very opposite of meekness: sulking. Someone had hurt me. He/she was the one who needed to be changed! I felt I was misunderstood, unfairly treated, and unduly berated. Although I managed to keep my mouth shut, both the Lord and I knew that my thoughts did not spring from a depth of loving-kindness and holy charity. I wanted to vindicate myself to the offender. That was a revelation of how little I knew of meekness.

The Spirit of God reminded me that it was He who had provided this very thing to bring that lesson of meekness which I could learn nowhere else. He was literally putting me on the spot: would I choose, here and now, to *learn of Him*, learn *His* meekness? He was despised, rejected, reviled, pierced, crushed, oppressed, afflicted, yet He did not open His mouth. What was this little incident of mine by comparison with my Lord's suffering? He brought to mind Jesus' willingness not only to eat with Judas who would soon betray Him, but also to kneel before him and wash his dirty feet. He showed me the look the Lord gave Peter when he had three times denied Him—a look of unutterable love and forgiveness, a look of meekness which overpowered Peter's cowardice and selfishness, and brought him to repentance. I thought of His meekness as He hung pinioned on the cross, praying even in His agony for His Father's forgiveness for His killers. There was no venom or bitterness there, only the final proof of a sublime and invincible love.

But how shall I, not born with the smallest shred of that quality, I who love victory by argument and put-down, ever learn that holy meekness? The prophet Zephaniah tells us to *seek* it (Zephaniah 2:3). We must walk (live) in the Spirit, not gratifying the desires of the sinful nature (for example, my desire to answer back, to offer excuses and accusations, my desire to show up the other's fault instead of to be shown my own). We must "clothe" ourselves (Colossians 3:12) with meekness—put it on, like a garment. This entails an explicit choice: I will be meek. I will *not* sulk, will *not* retaliate, will *not* carry a chip.

A steadfast look at Jesus instead of at the injury makes a very great difference. Seeking to see things in His light changes the aspect altogether.

In *Pilgrim's Progress*, Prudence asks Christian in the House Beautiful, "Can you remember by what means you find your annoyances at times, as if they were vanquished?"

"Yes," says Christian, "when I think what I saw at the Cross, that will do it."

The message of the cross is foolishness to the world and to all whose thinking is still worldly. But "the foolishness of God is wiser than man's wisdom, and the weakness of God is stronger than man's strength" (1 Corinthians 1:25, NIV). The meekness of Jesus was a force more irresistible than any force on earth. "By the meekness and gentleness of Christ," wrote the great apostle, "I appeal to you.... Though we live in the world, we do not wage war as the world does. The weapons we fight with are not the weapons of the world. On the contrary, they have divine power to demolish strongholds" (2 Corinthians 10:1, 3-4, NIV). The weapon of meekness counters all enmity, says author Dietrich Von Hildebrand, with the offer of an unshielded heart.

Isn't this the simple explanation for our being so heavy-laden, so tired, so overburdened and confused and bitter? We drag around such prodigious loads of resentment and self-assertion. Shall we not rather accept at once the loving invitation: "Come to Me. Take My yoke. Learn of Me—I am gentle, meek, humble, lowly. I will give you rest" (Matthew 11:28-29 paraphrased).

The Weapon of Prayer

News came one day which indicated that a matter I had been praying about had deteriorated rather than improved. *What good are my prayers, anyway?* I was tempted to ask. Why bother? It's becoming a mere charade. But the words of Jesus occurred in my Bible reading that very morning (and wasn't it a good thing I'd taken time to hear Him?): "If you, bad as you are, know how to give your children what is good for them, how much more will your heavenly Father give good things to those who ask him?" (Matthew 7:11, NEB).

Are you as often tempted as I am to doubt the effectiveness of prayer? But Jesus prayed. He told us to pray. We can be sure that the answer will come, and it will be *good*. If it is not exactly what we expected, chances are we were not asking for quite the right thing. Our heavenly Father hears the prayer, but wants to give us bread rather than stones.

Prayer is a weapon. Paul speaks of the "weapons we wield" in 2 Corinthians 10:4-5. They are "not merely human, but divinely potent to demolish strongholds" (NEB). The source of my doubts about its potency that morning was certainly not the Holy Spirit. It was the unholy spirit, the Destroyer himself, urging me to quit using the weapon he fears so intensely.

∽∾∽

Why Bother to Pray?

If God is sovereign, and things will be as they are going to be anyway, why bother to pray? There are several reasons. The first is really all we *need* to know: God has told us to pray. It is a commandment, and if we love Him, we obey His commands.

Second, Jesus prayed. People sometimes say that the only reason for prayer is that *we* need to be changed. Certainly we do, but that is not the only reason to pray. Jesus did not need to be changed or made more holy by praying. He was communing with His Father. He asked for things. He thanked God. In His Gethsemane prayer, He besought His Father to prevent what was about to take place. He also laid down His own will.

Third, prayer is a law of the universe. God ordained that certain physical laws should govern the operation of this world. Books simply will not stay put on a table without the operation of the law of gravity. There are spiritual laws as well. Certain things will not happen without the operation of prayer. God could cause books to stay on tables by what theologians call "divine *fiat*." Everything we pray for could occur in the same way, but that is not how things were arranged. Pascal, the great French thinker, said that in prayer God gives us "the dignity of causality."

Bible reading should shape our prayers. Here is a passage from Colossians (3:12-14, PHILLIPS) which hits me between the eyes and shows me very clearly some changes I need God's help to make:

> As God's picked representatives of the new humanity, purified and beloved of God himself, be merciful in action, kindly in

heart, humble in mind. Accept life, and be most patient and tolerant with one another, always ready to forgive if you have a difference with anyone. Forgive as freely as the Lord has forgiven you. And, above everything else, be truly loving, for love is the golden chain of all the virtues.

CRYCRO

Prayer Is Conflict

Prayer is no easy pastime. As I grow old I find that I am more conscious than ever of my need to pray, but it seems at the same time to become more of a struggle. It is harder to concentrate, for one thing. I was greatly helped by some private notes Amy Carmichael wrote to her "Family" (hundreds of children and their helpers, both Indian and European) in Dohnavur, South India, to help them prepare for a special day of prayer.

She quoted Paul's letter to the Colossians (2:1, KJV): "I would that ye knew what great conflict I have for you." He is referring at least in part to the conflict of prayer. The same verse is translated "how greatly I strive" in the Revised Version; "how deep is my anxiety" in J.B. Phillips; and, in the Jerusalem Bible, "Yes, I want you to know that I do have to struggle hard for you... to bind you together in love and to stir your minds, so that your understanding may come to full development, until you really know God's secret in which all the jewels of wisdom and knowledge are hidden."

Here are Amy's notes:

With what did I struggle?

1. With all that says to me, what is the use of your praying? So many others, who know more of prayer than you do, are praying. What difference does it make whether you pray or not? Are you sure that your Lord is listening? Of course He is listening to the other prayers but yours are of such small account, are you really sure He is "bending His ear" to *you?*

2. With all that suggests that we are asked to give too much time to prayer. There is so much to do. Why set aside so much time just to pray?

3. With all that discourages me personally—perhaps the remembrance of past sin, perhaps spiritual or physical tiredness; with anything and everything that keeps me back from what occupied St. Paul so often—vital prayer.

What will help me most in this wrestle?

1. The certain knowledge that our insignificance does not matter at all, for we do not come to the Father in our own name but in the Name of His beloved Son. His ear is always open to that Name. Of this we can be certain.

2. The certain knowledge that this is Satan's lie; he is much more afraid of our prayer than our work. (This is proved by the immense difficulties we always find when we set ourselves to pray. They are much greater than those we meet when we set ourselves to work.)

3. Isaiah 44:22 and kindred words, with 1 John 1:9, meet all distress about sin. Isaiah 40:29-31 with 2 Corinthians 12:9,10 meets everything that spiritual or physical weariness can do to hinder. Psalm 27:8 with Isaiah 45:19 meets all other difficulties. And the moment we say to our God, "Thy face, Lord, will I seek," His mighty energies come to the rescue. (See Colossians 1:2, 9) *Greater, far greater, is He that is in us than he that is against us. Count on the greatness of God. But are we to go on wrestling to the end?*

No, there is a point to which we come, when, utterly trusting the promise of our Father, we rest our hearts upon Him. It is then we are given what St. Paul calls access with confidence (Ephesians 3:12). But don't forget that this access is by faith, not by feeling, faith in Him our living Lord; He who says "Come unto Me" does not push us away when we come. As we go on, led by the Holy Spirit who so kindly helps our infirmities, we find ourselves in 1 John 5:14, 15 and lastly in Philippians 4:6, 7. It is good to remember that immediate answer to prayer is not always something seen, but it is always inward peace.

And if the day ends otherwise and we are discouraged? Then tell Him so, "nothing ashamed of tears upon His feet" [here she is quoting from F.W.H. Meyers's poem "St. Paul"]. Lord, Thou knowest all things. Thou knowest that I love Thee. "Yes, my child, I know." But don't settle down into an "it will never be different" attitude. It *will* be different if only in earnest we follow on to know the Lord.

Be Honest with God

Since God knows our thoughts even before we think them, isn't it absurd of us to hesitate to tell Him the straight truth about ourselves? When we feel we ought to try to cover our spiritual nakedness it is good for us to open up Psalm 139: "O Lord, you have searched me and you know me.... You perceive my thoughts from afar.... You are familiar with all my ways. Before a word is on my tongue you know it completely, O Lord.... You created my inmost being" (Psalm 139:1-4, 13, NIV).

There are times when I hesitate even to pray, knowing how far short I fall from God's standard.

George MacDonald writes:

If I felt my heart as hard as a stone; if I did not love God, or man, or woman, or little child, I would yet say to God in my heart, "O God, see how I trust Thee, because Thou art perfect, and not changeable like me. I do not love Thee. I love nobody. I am not even sorry for it. Thou seest how much I need Thee to come close to me, to put Thy arm round me, to say to me, *my child*: for the worse my state, the greater my need of my Father who loves me. Come to me, and my day will dawn; my love will come back, and, oh! how I shall love Thee, my God! and know that my love is Thy love, my blessedness Thy being."

We may pray the prayer that closes Psalm 139: "Search me, O God, and know my heart; test me and know my anxious thoughts. See if there is any offensive way in me, and lead me in the way everlasting" (Psalm 139:23-24, NIV).

"Be persuaded, timid soul," writes Archbishop Fenelon, in his *Spiritual Letters to Women*, "that He has loved you too much to cease loving you."

An Old Prayer

Christians in the Orthodox Church use a prayer called the Jesus Prayer. Sometimes they pray it in the rhythm of breathing, learning in this way almost to "pray without ceasing." The words are simple, but they cover everything we need to ask for ourselves and others: *Lord Jesus Christ, Son of God, have mercy on us.*

The Lord did not say we should not use repetition. He said we should not use vain repetition. A prayer prayed from the heart of the child to the Father is never vain.

The Very Reverend Kenneth R. Waldron, a priest of both the Ukrainian Orthodox Church and of the Anglican Church, wrote to me of his having had surgery. "The last moment of consciousness before the anaesthetic took over, I heard my surgeon repeating in a whisper: GOSPODI POMILUY, GOSPODI POMILUY, GOSPODI POMILUY [Dr. Waldron put the Russian words into phonetic spelling]—Lord, have mercy on us.... It is wonderful to drift off into unconsciousness hearing these words on the lips of the man whose hands you trust to bring you out of your troubles. It is great to have a surgeon who knows how to pray at such a time. Think of the comfort and help that this simple prayer has brought to thousands through the years, a prayer that was a big help to me in January 1982. Some of my hospital friends thought they would not see me alive again, but the good Lord had a bit more work for this old priest to do."

The Jesus Prayer was one my husband Add and I often used together when he was dying of cancer, when we seemed to have "used up" all the other prayers. I recommend it to you.

∽∽∽

Lost and Found

Here is a little story about a simple answer to prayer. Lars was away. I had to take the car to the repairman's house. Li Zeng, our live-in student, followed me in his car to bring me home. Directions to the house had been ambiguous, and Gloucester, Massachusetts gets the prize for town-easiest-to-get-lost-in. I prayed that I might not get lost—Li had to get to class, the repairman had to leave at 7:15. I got lost, made a quick turn without checking to see that Li was still with me. He wasn't. "Lord, Li will be late for class, the man will leave in a few minutes—what shall I do?" It's a long story, but after a phone call I found the house, left the car, declined the man's kind offer to take me home because I wanted to find Li so he would not miss his class. How was I to find him? "Lord, help me." I stood at an intersection and prayed that he would come along—an absurd request in a place like Gloucester. He'd been on a one-way street which would take him far out around the shore drive, with no reason to happen upon the intersection where I stood. Within five minutes there he was! God teaches us to ask so that He may answer our prayers. This reminds us of the source of our blessings. The answer to my prayer *not* to get lost was No—*in order that I might be specially blessed in the way I was found.*

Remember how the Lord brought Israel *out* (of Egypt) in order to bring them *in* (to Canaan)? He got me lost that He might get me found! Let's never forget that some of His greatest mercies are His refusals. He says no in order that He may, in some way we cannot imagine, say yes. All His ways with us are merciful. His meaning is always love.

After I had written the above, I received the following much more astonishing story from Brenda Foltz of Princeton, Minnesota. She went rock-climbing for the first time:

> I started up the rock as fast as I could, determined to "set my face like a flint" toward the peak. After a time, I came to a difficult ledge, and my breathless scrambling came to an abrupt halt. Suddenly, the rope was pulled too taut and hit me square in the eye. "Oh NO!" I thought wildly, "my contact lens is GONE!" From my precarious perch I looked everywhere on the rope and sharp granite rock for a tiny, transparent lens, which could easily be mistaken for a water droplet.
>
> "Lord Jesus, help me find it!" I prayed and pleaded, knowing the hopelessness of my search with such limited mobility. I looked as long as I could maintain my hold, praying with a sinking heart. Finally I resumed my climb with one last glimmer of hope—maybe the contact was still in my eye, crumpled in the corner or up under my eyelid. When I reached the top, I had a friend check to see if she could find it in my eye. It wasn't there. Every hope was gone.
>
> I was disappointed, and anxious about getting a new contact so far away from home. As we sat and rested, surveying the world from such a gloriously high perspective, the fragment of a verse popped into my head: "The eyes of God go to and fro through the whole earth."
>
> God knows *exactly where my contact is* this moment from His high vantage point, the amazing thought struck me. But *I'll* never see it again, I concluded.
>
> So, still glum, I headed down the path to the bottom where the others were preparing to climb. About half an hour later another girl set out where I had also begun my climb. She had no inkling of the missing contact. But there, at the steep bottom of the rock face, she let out an excited cry: "Hey you guys—did anyone lose a contact?"

I rushed over as she continued yelling, "There's an ANT carrying a contact down the mountain!"

Sure enough. Special delivery! I bent down, retrieved my contact from the hardworking ant, doused it with water and put it back in my eye, rejoicing. I was in awe, as if my Father had just given me, though so undeserving, a big hug, and said, "My precious daughter, I care about *every* detail of your life."

I wrote to tell my family. My dad drew a cartoon portraying an ant, lugging a big contact five times its size. The ant was saying to God, "Lord, I don't understand why You want me to drag this thing down! What use is it anyway? I don't even know what it is, and I certainly can't eat it and it's so BIG and HEAVY. Oh well, if you say so, Lord, I'll try, but it seems like a useless piece of junk to me!"

I marvel at God's ways and how He chooses to reveal His mercy in ways *far beyond* our human comprehension.

∞∞

We should all endeavor and labor for a calmer spirit, that we may the better serve God in praying to Him and praising Him; and serve one another in love, that we may be fitted to do and receive good; that we may make our passage to heaven more easy and cheerful, without drooping and hanging the wing. So much as we are quiet and cheerful upon good ground, so much we live, and are, as it were, in heaven.

R. Sibbes

∞∞

Thanksgiving for What is Given

S ome people are substituting "Turkey Day" for Thanksgiving. I guess it must be because they are not aware that there's anybody to thank, and they think that the most important thing about the holiday is food. Christians know there is Somebody to thank, but often when we make a list of things to thank Him for we include only things we like. A bride and groom can't get away with that. They write a note to everybody, not only the rich uncle who gave the couple matching BMWs, but the poor aunt who gave them a crocheted toilet-paper cover. In other words, they have to express thanks for whatever they've received.

Wouldn't that be a good thing for us to do with God? We are meant to give thanks "in everything" even if we're like the little girl who said she could think of a lot of things she'd rather have than eternal life. The mature Christian offers not just polite thanks but heartfelt thanks that springs from a far deeper source than his own pleasure. Thanksgiving is a spiritual exercise, necessary to the building of a healthy soul. It takes us out of the stuffiness of ourselves into the fresh breeze and sunlight of the will of God. The simple act of thanking Him is for most of us an abrupt change of activity, a break from work and worry, a move toward re-creation.

I am not suggesting the mouthing of foolish platitudes, or evasion of the truth. That is not how God is glorified, or souls fortified. I want to see clearly what I have been given and to thank Him with an honest heart. What are the "givens"?

Thankless children we all are, more or less, comprehending but dimly the truth of God's fathomless love for us. We do not know Him as a gracious Giver, we do not understand His most precious gifts, or the depth of His love, the wisdom with which He has planned our lives, the price He pays to bring us to glory and fulfillment. When some petty private concern or perhaps some bad news depresses or confuses me, I am in no position to be thankful. Far from it. That is the time, precisely then, that I must begin by deliberately putting my mind on some great Realities.

What are these "givens"? What do I most unshakably believe in? God the Father Almighty. Jesus Christ His only Son. The Holy Ghost, the holy catholic Church, the communion of saints, the forgiveness of sins, the resurrection of the body, the life everlasting. Not a long list, but all we need. "The necessary supplies issued to us, the standard equipment of the Christian." We didn't ask for any of them. (Imagine having nothing more than we've asked for!) They are *given*.

Take the list of whatever we're not thankful for and measure it against the mighty foundation stones of our faith. The truth of our private lives can be understood only in relation to those Realities. Some of us know very little of suffering, but we know disappointments and betrayals and losses and bitterness. Are we really meant to thank God for such things? Let's be clear about one thing: God does not *cause* all the things we don't like. But He does permit them to happen because it is in this fallen world that we humans must learn to walk by faith. He doesn't leave us to ourselves, however. He shares every step. He walked this lonesome road first, He gave Himself for us, He died for us. "Can we not trust such a God to give us, with Him, everything else that we can need?" (Romans 8:32, PHILLIPS). Those disappointments give us the chance to learn to know Him and the meaning of His gifts, and, in the midst of darkness, to receive His light. Doesn't *that* transform the not-thankful list into a thankful one?

A New Thanksgiving

Those who call Thanksgiving "Turkey Day," I suppose, take some such view as this: Unless we have Someone to thank and something to thank Him for, what's the point of using a name that calls up pictures of religious people in funny hats and Indians bringing corn and squash? Christians, I hope, focus on something other than a roasted bird. We do have Someone to thank and a long list of things to thank Him for, but sometimes we limit our thanksgiving merely to things that look good to us. As our faith in the character of God grows deeper we see that heavenly light is shed on everything—even on suffering—so that we are enabled to thank Him for things we would never have thought of before. The apostle Paul, for example, saw even suffering itself as a happiness (Colossians 1:24, NEB).

I have been thinking of something that stifles thanksgiving. It is the spirit of greed—the greed of doing, being, and having.

When Satan came to tempt Jesus in the wilderness, his bait was intended to inspire the lust to do more than the Father meant for Him to do—to go farther, demonstrate more power, act more dramatically. So the enemy comes to us in these days of frantic *doing*. We are ceaselessly summoned to activities: social, political, educational, athletic, and—yes—spiritual. Our "self-image" (deplorable word!) is dependent not on the quiet and hidden "Do this for My sake," but on the list the world hands us of what is "important." It is a long list, and it is both foolish and impossible. If we fall for it, we neglect the short list.

Only a few things are really important, and for those we have the promise of divine help: sitting in silence with the Master in order to hear His word and obey it in the ordinary line of *duty*—for example, in being a good husband, wife, father, mother, son, daughter, or *spiritual* father or mother to those nearby who need protection and care—humble work which is never on the world's list because it leads to nothing impressive on one's resumé. As Washington Gladden wrote in 1879, "O Master, let me walk with Thee/ In *lowly* paths of service free...."

Temptation comes also in the form of *being*. The snake in the garden struck at Eve with the promise of being something which had not been given. If she would eat the fruit forbidden to her, she could "upgrade her lifestyle" and become like God. She inferred that this was her right, and that God meant to cheat her of this. The way to get her rights was to disobey Him.

No new temptation ever comes to any of us. Satan needs no new tricks. The old ones have worked well ever since the Garden of Eden, although sometimes under different guises. When there is a deep restlessness for which we find no explanation, it may be due to the greed of *being*—what our loving Father never meant us to be. Peace lies in the trusting acceptance of His design, His gifts, His appointment of place, position, capacity. It was thus that the Son of Man came to earth—embracing all that the Father willed Him to be, usurping nothing—no work, not even a *word*—that the Father had not given Him.

Then there is the greed of having. When "a mixed company of strangers" joined the Israelites, the people began to be greedy for better things (Numbers 11:4, NEB). God had given them exactly what they needed in the wilderness: manna. It was always enough, always fresh, always good (sounds good to me, anyway, "like butter-cakes"). But the people lusted for variety. These strangers put ideas into their heads. "There's more to life than this stuff. Is *this* all you've got? You can have more. You gotta live a little!"

So the insistence to have it all took hold on God's people and they began to wail, "all of them in their families at the opening of their tents." There is no end to the spending, getting, having. We are insatiable consumers, dead set on competing, upgrading, showing off ("If you've got it, flaunt it"). We simply cannot bear to miss something others deem necessary. So the world ruins the peace and simplicity God would give us. Contentment with what He has chosen for us dissolves, along with godliness, while, instead of giving thanks, we lust and wail, teaching our children to lust and wail too. (Children of the jungle tribe I knew years ago did not complain *because they had not been taught to.*)

Lord, we give You thanks for all that You in Your mercy have given us to be and to do and to have. Deliver us, Lord, from all greed to be and to do and to have anything not in accord with Your holy purposes. Teach us to rest quietly in Your promise to supply, recognizing that if we don't have it we don't need it. Teach us to desire Your will—nothing more, nothing less, and nothing else. For Jesus' sake. Amen.

ᏫᏫᎦ

An Overflowing Cup

//"The Lord is gracious and compassionate.: good to all... faithful to all his promises... loving toward all he has made.... righteous in all his ways.... near to all who call on him.... watches over all who love him.... My mouth will speak in praise of the Lord" (from Psalm 145, NIV).

As the year dwindles my heart swells. How to express the joy and gratitude for daily evidence of all the above? I thank God for all the saints whose lives have demonstrated to me what it means to be a Christian. Dr. May Powell, a remarkable English lady, died at age ninety-five. She had joined Amy Carmichael in her work in India in 1924, helping to build up the medical work and then, when Amy was injured, becoming co-leader with her of the Dohnavur Fellowship. After Amy's death in 1951 the responsibility of leader fell to Dr. Powell. Eventually, she returned to England to care for two older sisters. Following their deaths she continued to serve the Lord she loved, always available to many who needed her prayers and her counsel.

I visited her in England in 1983 when I was working on *A Chance to Die*, the biography of Amy Carmichael. She had given me specific instructions by phone as to train, taxi, and finding the residential home where she lived. She was waiting at the door, very tiny and erect, very cheerful and direct, reminding me at once (but in appearance *only*) of the old lady in "Beverly Hillbillies"!

"So you're Elisabeth. Come in. Do you know the word loo? (I did—British nickname for toilet.) Yes. There's the loo. There's your room. Tea at the top of these stairs in twenty minutes." Up the stairs she went with great energy. Her room was not much more than a cell. A narrow cot, a small table with the teakettle, cups and biscuits all ready on a neat cloth, two chairs. A short bookshelf on the wall. Half of the books were Amy Carmichael's. I had my notebook in hand.

"What would you like to know?" she asked. There wasn't time for nearly all my questions, but in those hours I knew that I had been with a very great woman, one of God's hidden ones whose strength lies in nothing explainable by personality or heredity, but in Him who is Rock, Fortress, and Might, who is, "in the darkness drear their one true light," whose distant song of triumph steals on our ears sometimes and makes our hearts brave again and our arms strong. Praise to God for such living flames of His love.

And then there are my parents, both of whom are now also with the Lord, but with whom I feel that I have been living again during the past year as I worked on a book on the shaping of one Christian family. Studying minutely their letters and diaries, rereading the autobiography Mother wrote for us children, poring over the pictures, ransacking my memory and the memories of my brothers and sister, I have often paused and said, "Thank You," to Him who gave us such parents and such a home. I have also been solemnly aware of the weight of responsibility that is laid upon us because "to whomsoever much is given much is required."

As an editor my father spent his life reading other people's writings and never thought of writing a book. Three collections of his short writings were published in book form, however, one entitled *New Every Morning* (published by Zondervan in 1969, now out of print). Here's the title piece, an exercise in thanksgiving, and a glimpse of the man he was. I think you'll see why I'm thankful for such a father:

"Blessings taken for granted are often forgotten. Yet our Heavenly Father 'daily loadeth us with benefits' (Psalm 68:19). Think of some of the common things which are nevertheless wonderful:

"—the intricate, delicate mechanism of the lungs steadily and silently taking in fresh air eighteen to twenty times a minute;

"—the untiring heart, pumping great quantities of clean blood through the labyrinth of blood vessels;

"—the constant body temperature, normally varying less than one degree;

"—the atmospheric temperature, varying widely it is true, but never so much as to destroy human and animal life;

"—the orderly succession of day and night, spring, summer, autumn, and winter, so that, with few exceptions, man can make his plans accordingly;

"—the great variety of foods, from the farm, the field, the forest, and the sea, to suit our differing desires and physical needs;

"—the beauties of each day—the morning star and growing light of sunrise, the white clouds of afternoon, the soft tints of a peaceful sunset, and the glory of the starry heavens;

"—the symphony of early morning bird songs, ranging from the unmusical trill of the chipping sparrow to the lilting ecstasy of the goldfinch and the calm, rich, bell-like tones of the wood and hermit thrushes;

"—the refreshment that sleep brings;

"—the simple joys of home—the children's laughter and whimsical remarks, happy times around the table, the love and understanding of husband and wife, and the harmony of voices raised together in praise to God.

"All these and many others come from the bountiful hand of Him 'who redeemeth thy life from destruction; who crowneth thee with lovingkindness and tender mercies; who satisfieth thy mouth with good things; so that thy youth is renewed like the eagle's' (Psalm 103:4,5).

"'It is of the Lord's mercies that we are not consumed, because His compassions fail not. They are new every morning: great is thy faithfulness' (Lamentations 3:22,23).

"'It is a good thing to give thanks unto the Lord, and to sing praises unto thy name, O most High' (Psalm 92:1)."

Hints for Quiet Time

Having a quiet time with the Lord every day is absolutely essential if you expect to grow spiritually. But you have to plan it. It won't "just happen." We're all much too busy. Early morning is best, and there are plenty of scriptural precedents for that (Jesus rose "a great while before day"; the psalmist said, "In the morning shalt Thou hear my voice"). If you meet the Lord before you meet anybody else, you'll be "pointed in the right direction" for whatever comes. God knows how difficult it is for some to do this, and if you have a reason you can offer *Him* why early morning won't work, I'm sure He'll help you to find another time. Sometimes the children's afternoon nap time can be quiet time for a mother. At any rate, plan the time. Make up your mind to stick with it. Make it short to begin with—fifteen minutes or so, perhaps. You'll be surprised at how soon you'll be wanting more.

Take a single book of the Bible. If you're new at this, start with the Gospel of Mark. Pray, first, for the Holy Spirit's teaching. Read a few verses, a paragraph, or a chapter. Then ask, What does this passage teach me about: (1) God, (2) Jesus Christ, (3) the Holy Spirit, (4) myself, (5) sins to confess or avoid, (6) commands to obey, (7) what Christian love is?

Keep a notebook. Write down some of your special prayer requests with the date. Record the answer when it comes. Note, also, some of the answers you've found to the above questions, or anything else you've learned. Tell your children, your spouse, your friends some of these things. That will help you to remember them. You'll be amazed at what a difference a quiet time will make in your life.

Chronicle of a Soul

I kept a five-year diary from high school through college, and began spiritual journals during my senior year in college (1948), which I continue to keep. These are chronicles of growth: mental, emotional, and spiritual. It is astounding to go back through them and learn things I had completely forgotten. It is wonderfully faith-strengthening to see that indeed "all the way my Savior leads me," hears my prayers, supplies my needs, teaches me of Himself. As God said to Israel, "Thou shalt *remember* all the way which the Lord thy God led these forty years in the wilderness."

My memory is poor. A journal is a record of His faithfulness (and my own faithlessness too—which teaches me to value His grace and mercy). If you decide to begin recording your pilgrimage, buy yourself a notebook (or one of those pretty flowered cloth-bound blank books available in gift and stationery stores) and begin to put down (not necessarily every day):

1. Lessons learned from your reading of Scripture. (If you put these in a journal instead of marking up your Bible, you will find new things each time you read the Bible instead of reading it through the grid of old notes. Worth a try?)

2. Ways in which you intend to apply those lessons in your own life. (Reading your journal later will reveal answers to prayer you would otherwise have overlooked.)

3. Dialogues with the Lord. What you say to Him, what He seems to be saying to you about some problem or issue or need.

4. Quotations from your spiritual reading other than the Bible.

5. Prayers from the words of hymns which you want to make your own.

6. Reasons for thanksgiving. (Caution: when you get into the habit of recording these, the list gets out of hand!)

7. Things you're praying about. You might choose to have a separate notebook for this, or an "appendix" in another section of the same book—date on which a prayer was prayed; date on which answered, with space for *how* the answer came in some cases.

If you have a family, I would strongly urge you as a family to keep a prayer notebook together. This will help everybody first of all to learn to *pray* about *everything*, instead of merely talking or worrying or arguing. It will also help you to be specific, to hold your requests before the Lord together, and then to note the answers and give thanks together (especially when the answers weren't the ones you were looking for).

As George MacDonald wrote, "No gift unrecognized as coming from God is at its own best: therefore many things that God would gladly give us, things even that we need because we are, must wait until we ask for them, that we may know whence they come: when in all gifts we find Him, then in Him we shall find all things."

Where I found Truth, there I found my God, the Truth itself, which since I learnt, I have not forgotten.... Too late I loved Thee, O Thou Beauty of ancient days, yet ever new! too late I loved Thee! And behold, Thou wert within, and I abroad, and there I searched for Thee... Thou calledst, and shoutedst, and burstest my deafness. Thou flashedst, shonest, and scatteredst my blindness. Thou breathedst odors, and *I drew in breath* and *pant for Thee.* I tasted, and *hunger and thirst.* Thou touchedst me, and I burned for Thy peace.

Confessions, St. Augustine (italics his)

He who believes in God is not careful for the morrow, but labors joyfully and with a great heart. "For He giveth His beloved, as in sleep." They must work and watch, yet never be careful or anxious, but commit all to Him, and live in serene tranquillity; and with a quiet heart, as one who sleeps safely and quietly.

Martin Luther

⚭⚭

Waiting

"I waited patiently for the Lord; he turned to me and heard my cry" (Psalm 40:1, NIV).

The tests of our willingness to wait patiently for the Lord come almost daily for most of us, I suppose. Probably I am among the Lord's most *impatient* servants, so the lesson has to be reviewed again and again. A tough test came when my daughter's family (of ten) was searching for a house. Southern California is not a place where one would wish to conduct that search. It's a long story, but at last, all other possibilities having been exhausted, a house was found, an offer made. That night word came that two other offers, of unknown amounts, had also been made. Dark pictures filled my mind: the others would surely get the house, the Shepards would be reduced to renting and we'd been told that rentals start at about $2000 per month (imagine an owner willing to rent to a family with eight children!).

"Wait for the Lord; be strong and take heart and wait for the Lord" (Psalm 27:14, NIV).

I lay awake in the wee hours ("when all life's molehills become mountains" as Amy Carmichael said), repeating Scripture about God's faithfulness, trusting, casting all cares, waiting. I had to keep offering up my worries and my impatience. At four I was up reading the story of Abraham and Isaac. Abraham called the place where he had offered up Isaac "The Lord Will Provide." I took that as the Lord's word to me that morning.

Before nine o'clock, my son-in-law Walt called to say "Offer accepted. Other offers, both *higher*, turned down." No explanation. It was the Lord's doing.

Waiting requires patience—a willingness calmly to accept what we have or have not, where we are or where we wish we were, whomever we live or work with.

To want what we don't have is impatience, for one thing, and it is to mistrust God. Is He not in complete control of all circumstances, events, and conditions? If some are beyond His control, He is not God.

A spirit of resistance cannot wait on God. I believe it is this spirit which is the reason for some of our greatest sufferings. Opposing the workings of the Lord in and through our "problems" only exacerbates them. It is *here* and *now* that we must win our victories or suffer defeats. Spiritual victories are won in the quiet acceptance of ordinary events, which are God's "bright servants," standing all around us.

Restlessness and impatience change nothing except our peace and joy. Peace does not dwell in outward things, but in the heart prepared to wait trustfully and quietly on Him who has *all* things safely in His hands. "Peace I leave with you; I do not give to you as the world gives" (John 14:27, NEB). What sort of peace has He to give us? A peace which was constant in the midst of ceaseless work (with few visible results), frequent interruptions, impatient demands, few physical comforts; a peace which was not destroyed by the arguments, the faithlessness, and hatred of the people. Jesus had perfect confidence in His Father, whose will He had come to accomplish. Nothing touched Him without His Father's permission. Nothing touches me without my Father's permission. Can I not then wait patiently? He will show the way.

If I am willing to be still in my Master's hand, can I not then be still in everything? He's got the whole world *in His hands!* Never mind whether things come from God Himself or from people— everything comes by His ordination or permission. If I mean to be obedient and submissive to the Lord because He *is* my Lord, I must not forget that whatever He allows to happen becomes, for *me,* His will at that moment. Perhaps it is someone else's sinful action, but if God allows it to affect me, He wills it for my learning. The need to *wait* is, for me, a form of chastening. God has to calm me down, make me shut up and look to Him for the outcome.

His message to me every day
Is wait, be still, trust, and obey.

And this brings me to the matter of counseling. Upon our return from a trip to England I found a pile of mail, so many letters asking me what to do about things, for example: a wife's critical spirit, unemployment, a wife who has abandoned husband and children, a single mother doing a job she hates, an unfaithful husband, a woman (who tells me she is Spirit-filled) having an affair with her pastor, a farmer who'd like a wife, a mother-in-law who is nasty to her daughter-in-law, a stepson who is angry because "we don't spend enough money on his children," a wife who snaps at her husband each time he tries to snuggle up, and a husband who "drinks like a fish, curses like a sailor, and says he loves God."

I wish I could write the same letter to everybody: Wait patiently for the Lord. He will turn to you and hear your cry. It is amazing how clear things become when we are *still* before Him, not complaining, not insisting on quick answers, only seeking to hear His word in the stillness, and to see things in His light. Few are willing to receive that sort of reply. "Too simplistic" is the objection. One listener to my radio program, *Gateway to Joy*, wrote, "I got so upset at what you were saying I ripped the earphones out and said, 'I'll do what I want to do!'" But there are those who can say, "This is the Lord; we have waited for him, we will be glad and rejoice in his salvation" (Isaiah 25:9, KJV). Here are two testimonies:

"I've lost my mother, my brother, my husband, and my baby. My song is *More Love to Thee, O Christ.*"

"God picked up the scraps and pieces and made us whole—a whole woman, a whole man, a whole marriage."

CRCRCD

God's Sheep-Dogs

F rom a friend whose son, two and a half, had to have surgery for a cyst (always a worrisome sign): "The cyst was benign! We are so grateful! We set the Lord before us so we will not be shaken for the living of life. Our goal is not to be comfortable and have everything turn out fine, but to be godly and make an impact on our dying world and its values.... May God continue to refine your life message as 'he keeps you from willful sins as His servant; may they not rule over you' (Psalm 19:13). Barrett (my son) memorized Genesis 4:7, and as he faces temptation he says the verse. He is learning to make wise choices and to be obedient.... We have not spared the rod on him but it has really worked. He says 'the rod drives out my foolishness.'"

That letter came on the same day that I was reading Hannah Whitall Smith's *Everyday Religion*. She quotes George MacDonald. His words illuminate what Barrett's mother wrote:

"Man has a claim on God, a divine claim for any pain, want, disappointment, or misery that will help to make him what he ought to be. He has a claim to be punished, and to be spared not one pang that may urge him toward repentance; yea, he has a claim to be compelled to repent; to be hedged in on every side, to have one after another of the strong, sharp-toothed sheep-dogs of the Great Shepherd sent after him, to thwart him in any desire, foil him in any plan, frustrate him of any hope, until he comes to see at length that nothing will ease his pain, nothing make life a thing worth having, but the presence of the living God within him; that nothing is good but the will of God; nothing noble enough for the desire of the heart of man but oneness with the eternal. For this God must make him yield his very being, that He himself may enter in and dwell with him."

Common Courtesy

Talking with a group of seminary students I mentioned that the common rules of courtesy are often overlooked nowadays, especially by those who grew up in the past two decades, an era in which all conventions and traditions were suspect. "Mere convention" came to mean "pure hypocrisy." If a thing was labelled "traditional," it had to be discarded as no longer "relevant," "meaningful," or even intelligent. If a man had the temerity to hold a door open for a woman, he was sometimes labelled "sexist." My point in bringing up the subject of courtesy was simply that it is a small way of demonstrating that deep principle, central to our Christian faith, of "my life for yours." I asked if any of the husbands in the room made a habit of helping their wives into their chairs at the table, even when company was not present. A week later one of the men stopped me in the seminary hall.

"I just want to tell you that my behavior toward my wife has been altered since last week's lecture. And you know what! It's changed my attitude toward her as well as hers toward me. It's really been revelatory! Just wanted to say thanks."

I was immensely cheered. It's always cheering to know somebody has had ears to hear, and has actually done something about what he's heard.

ᏯᎣᏯᎣᏯᎣ

Interruptions, Delays, Inconveniences

Emily, wife of America's first foreign missionary, Adoniram Judson, wrote home from Moulmein, Burma, in January 1847:

"This taking care of teething babies, and teaching natives to darn stockings and talking English back end foremost... in order to get an eatable dinner, is really a very odd sort of business for Fanny Forester [her penname—she was a well-known New England writer before marrying Judson].... But I begin to get reconciled to my minute cares." She was ambitious for "higher and better things," but was enabled to learn that "the person who would do great things well must practice daily on little ones; and she who would have the assistance of the Almighty in important acts, must be daily and hourly accustomed to consult His will in the minor affairs of life."

About eighty years ago, when James O. Fraser was working as a solitary missionary in Tengyueh, southwest China, his situation was, "in every sense, 'against the grain,'" He did not enjoy housekeeping and looking after premises. He found the houseboy irritable and touchy, constantly quarreling with the cook. Endless small items of business cluttered up the time he wanted for language study, and he was having to learn to be "perpetually inconvenienced" for the sake of the gospel. He wrote after some weeks alone:

> I am finding out that it is a mistake to plan to get through a certain amount of work in a certain time. It ends in disappoint-

ment, besides not being the right way to go about it, in my judgment. It makes one impatient of interruptions and delay. Just as you are nearly finishing—somebody comes along to sit with you and have a chat! You might hardly think it possible to be impatient and put out where there is such an opportunity for presenting the Gospel—but it is. It may be just on mealtime, or you are writing a letter to catch the mail, or you were just going out for needed exercise before tea. But the visitor has to be welcomed, and I think it is well to cultivate an attitude of mind which will enable one to welcome him from the heart and at any time. "No admittance except on business" scarcely shows a true missionary spirit.

There is nothing like the biographies of great Christians to give us perspective and help us to keep spiritual balance. These two are well worth reading. It was J.O. Fraser who so inspired my husband Jim Elliot with missionary vision that Jim planned to name his first son after him.

One more quotation—this from an out-of-print book, *The Life and Letters of Janet Erskine Stuart.* Says one who was her assistant for some years, "She delighted in seeing her plan upset by unexpected events, saying that it gave her great comfort, and that she looked on such things as an assurance that God was watching over her stewardship, was securing the accomplishment of His will, and working out His own designs. Whether she traced the secondary causes to the prayer of a child, to the imperfection of an individual, to obstacles arising from misunderstandings, or to interference of outside agencies, she was joyfully and graciously ready to recognize the indication of God's ruling hand, and to allow herself to be guided by it."

∽∽∽

My Life for Yours

About ten years ago, a young Canadian woman sat in the assembly hall at the University of Illinois in Urbana, along with seventeen thousand other students attending InterVarsity's missionary convention. She thrilled to the singing of the great hymns, led by Bernie Smith. She heard the speakers. "I remember the incredible excitement and desire to know and serve God that I experienced at that time. Now I have walked through some deep waters, and I feel compelled to write to you," her letter to me said. She had read two of my books just before the convention, and I happened to have been among the speakers. Another was Helen Roseveare, author of *Give Me This Mountain* and other books. At the time, Barbara was especially moved by the thought of the cost of declaring God's glory. Her letter told me this story:

Three years after Urbana she married Gerry Fuller, "a wonderful man who demonstrated zeal for Christ, a passion for souls, a beautiful compassion for hurting, broken people who needed to know the healing love of Jesus Christ." Following seminary and student pastorates, he became a prison chaplain and an inner-city missionary. Then he married Barbara and together they worked in Saint John, New Brunswick, with street kids, ex-convicts, and glue-sniffers.

The time came when Barbara saw Gerry seeking the Lord with such great intensity it made her question her own commitment to Christ. Was she prepared to die to self as he was? What was it that drove him to pray as he did—at least once until four in the morning? Was her own love for the Lord as deep as his, or was it perhaps shadowed by her love for her husband?

Gerry had a nephew named Gary, "a quiet guy with an artistic nature and talents that had been squelched as a child, leaving him very insecure, undisciplined." He couldn't hold down a job, got in trouble with the law. When relatives consented to his using their vacation cottage, a neighboring cottage was broken into. The owner called Gerry to say that his gun had been taken; Gary was the prime suspect, but they didn't want to call the police until they'd called Gerry.

Gerry was "scared stiff," but knew what he had to do the next day; put his whole trust in God, go to the cottage, try to persuade his nephew to turn himself in. He and Barbara went to bed.

Next morning when they prayed together he asked the Holy Spirit especially to strengthen Barbara in raising little Josh and Ben. Should she go with him to see Gary? She was relieved that his answer was no—"If anything happens to him, the children will need me," was the thought that flashed into her mind.

Gerry said goodbye. Barbara fasted, prayed, cared for the little boys, worked in the garden, waited. All day she waited. He did not come. Oh well, Gerry was always late for everything. No doubt they were deep in conversation. He had tried so often to help Gary. Lord, may He help him now.

At last the sound of a car. Eagerly Barbara looked up from her weeding. It was the Royal Canadian Mounted Police. She froze, then fell to the ground sobbing. Gerry was dead. But looking up at the bewildered faces of her sons, four and two years old, she pulled herself together, took their little hands, and told them Daddy was with Jesus and they wouldn't see him again for a long time. "From that point on there was the sense of being carried through the whole dream-like event. God surrounded me with His presence and an overwhelming sense that 'It's all right.' I knew He was in charge."

The murder was a deliberate act. Gary is serving a life sentence in a penitentiary with some who were led to Christ through Gerry's witness. They loved Gerry, but for love of his Lord they have forgiven his killer. A number of lives have been changed as a result of his testimony, but "in spite of the good things that came of his death there is always the WHY," Barbara writes. "As you say, we must let God be God. It's hard to explain, though, to a tired three-year-old when he wails, 'I miss Daddy!'

"One of my greatest blessings and comforts came as a surprise about six weeks after my husband's death when I discovered that I was pregnant with a baby conceived the eve of his homegoing. And how like the Lord and His perfect timing to present me with a beautiful child on Easter Sunday—the girl I had prayed for. Her name is Marah Grace and it is by God's grace that she has made my bitter waters sweet.

"People say I am brave, but I don't see any great bravery in walking through one of the difficult experiences of life. God is the One who strengthens us *at the time* for the things we must face. My greatest fear was the fear of losing Gerry, but when the time came God swooped under me as a great bird and carried me on eagle's wings above the storm.

"So that is my story. I wanted to share it with you—I feel somewhat akin to you. My husband went in obedience to God, well aware of the danger, and laid down his life for Christ's sake. My task is to follow that example and to instill in my children the values Gerry and I shared: the supreme value of knowing Jesus Christ and serving Him with our whole selves."

Thank you, dear Barbara, for being one more faithful witness to a wholly faithful and sovereign Lord. Like Jim Elliot, Gerry knew that "he is no fool who gives what he cannot keep to gain what he cannot lose." He would have understood the motto of the Coast Guard: "You have to go out, you don't have to come back."

Visit to Dohnavur

Because I had been invited to write a new biography of Amy Carmichael of Dohnavur, Lars and I visited the work she founded in South India. We arrived on their monthly prayer day in time to attend the evening meeting. The House of Prayer is a beautiful terra-cotta-colored building with a red tile roof and a tower which holds the chimes that play a hymn at 6:00 A.M. and 9:00 P.M. There is no furniture inside except a few chairs for older ones and decrepit foreigners such as we who aren't used to sitting on the floor. Everyone filed in in perfect silence, bare feet moving noiselessly over polished red tile floors, and sat in rows according to age, the tiny ones up front, dressed in brightly colored cotton dresses. Behind them sat the next age group, girls in skirts and blouses; then came those in skirts, blouses, and half-saris; finally the *accals* (older ones who look after the younger) in blue or purple or green saris. All had smoothly combed and oiled black hair, many of them with flowers in it. An Indian man played the little pump organ while they sang several traditional hymns in English, as well as songs written by "Amma" (the Tamil term of respect, used for Amy Carmichael). There was Scripture reading, then a prayer of thanksgiving for the new child who had just come, a little girl of two whose mother could not keep her. Her new mother, an *accal*, carried her to the platform and stood holding her while they prayed and then sang "Jesus Loves Me."

At another service in the House of Prayer, Lars and I sat in the tiny balcony which leads up to the tower. We looked down on the lovely scene, made even brighter this time because the smallest children had been given colored flags to wave in time to the music of certain songs; a custom instituted by Amma which I think should be adopted by every Sunday School and church, for it enables the tiny ones to participate by doing something even when they are too young to know the words by heart. Older ones played tambourines, triangle, and bells, while one drummed softly with a leather flap on the mouth of a clay pot.

I was allowed to use Amma's room for my reading and writing. Called the Room of Peace, it is spacious, has high ceilings and tiled floors, many doors and windows opening onto a verandah on three sides where there is a walk-in bird cage. A brick runway leads from the verandah to a platform under the trees where, following the accident which disabled her for the rest of her life, Amy Carmichael used to be taken to sit in the cool of the evening. Glass-doored bookcases, filled with her beloved books, stand around the walls of the room. Above them hang paintings of snowcaps by her friend, Dr. Howard Somervell, of Everest fame. There are hand-carved and painted wooden texts, "Good and Acceptable and Perfect" (referring to the lesson she found so hard to learn after the accident, of acceptance of the will of God), "A Very Present Help," "By one who loveth is another kindled" (from St. Augustine), and, the largest of all, blue letters on teak, "God hath not given us the spirit of fear." Also on the walls are a mounted tiger head, a pendulum clock, and one of the very few photographs ever taken of Amma.

In that Room of Peace I was glad not to be wearing shoes (nobody wears shoes in the houses of Dohnavur)—it seemed holy ground as I studied the marginal notes and underlinings of her favorite books, read the handwritten notebooks in which she explained for members of the Dohnavur Fellowship the "pattern shewn," the principles and practices which the Lord had given her at the inception of her work. I thumbed through worm-eaten ledgers, clippings, photographs—priceless documents that trace the day-by-day history of a task accepted for the Lord, the rescuing of little girls from temple prostitution and little boys from dramatic societies in which they were used for evil purposes. In later years the work included children in other kinds of need.

The most powerful witness to the quality of the service Amma rendered is to be seen in the Indian men and women who were reared there and who have remained to lay down their lives for others. Pungaja, for example, lives in the compound called Loving Place, where some of the mentally handicapped are cared for.

"I have no professional training," she told me. "The Holy Spirit gives me new wisdom each day to deal with them. Some are like wild animals, but the Lord Himself is my helper. I can't see on one side, but even in my weakness He has helped me. First Corinthians says that God has chosen the weak things of the world to confound the mighty, that no flesh should glory in his presence.

"One day I went to Amma with a burdened heart, but when she hugged me all my sorrow went.

"'What work are you doing?' Amma asked me. I told her.

"'Do you find it difficult?' I said yes.

"'These are soldiership years,' she said.

"Now it is my joy to serve these very difficult people."

She spoke quietly, looking out into the courtyard where some of them went back and forth. She had lost an eye as a child, and her face revealed suffering, but I saw the joy she spoke of written there, the joy of a laid-down life. I saw it in very many faces in Dohnavur. They do not mention that there are no diversions, no place to go, no time off (except two weeks per year—I asked about that). They do their work for Him who came not to be ministered unto.

We came away smitten, thinking of Amma's own words from her little book *If*, "...then I know nothing of Calvary love." The meaning of the living sacrifice, the corn of wheat, the crucified life, had been shown to us in twentieth century flesh and blood.

Neither go back in fear and misgiving to the past, nor in anxiety and forecasting to the future; but lie quiet under His hand, having no will but His.

H.E. Manning

∽∽∽

Regrets

When my father was twelve years old he lost his left eye through disobedience. He had been forbidden to have firecrackers, but he sneaked out early in the morning of July 4, 1910, and, with the help of a neighboring farmer, set off some dynamite caps. A piece of copper penetrated his eye.

Four years later my grandfather wrote this letter to my grandmother:

Dearest:

I am not one bit surprised that after all our experiences of the past four years you should suffer from sad memories, but I really do not believe for a moment that you should feel you have any occasion to let remorse bite into your life on account of Philip's accident. Surely we *cannot* guard against all the contingencies of this complex life, and no one who has poured out life as you have for each one of your children should let such regrets take hold.

None of us could be alive to the pressing needs of today if we should carry along with us the dark heaviness of *any* past, whether real or imagined. I know, dearest, that your Lord cannot wish anything of that sort for you, and I believe your steady, shining, and triumphant faith will lead you out through Him, into the richest experiences you have ever had. I *believe* that firmly.

I have had to turn to Him in helplessness today to overcome depression because of my failures. My Sunday School fiasco at

Swarthmore bears down pretty hard. But that is *not right.* I must look ahead, and up, as you often tell me, and *I will.* I know how sickening remorse is, if anyone knows; yet I also know, as you do, the lift and relief of turning the whole matter over to Him. We must have more prayers and more study together, dearest. I haven't followed the impulses I have so often had in this.

Lovingly, your own Phil.

My grandfather was the most cheerful and serene man I knew in my childhood. It is hard for me to imagine his having had any cause for remorse or temptation to depression. This letter, which bears a two-cent stamp and a Philadelphia postmark, was sent to Grandma in Franconia, New Hampshire, where they had a lovely vacation house. I spent my childhood summers in that house. I can picture her sitting on the porch, perhaps on the anniversary of her son's accident, looking out toward Mounts Lafayette, Bald, and Cannon, wrestling with the terrible thoughts of her own carelessness and failure. I thank God for my heritage. I thank Him for the word of His faithful servant Paul: "I concentrate on this: I leave the past behind and with hands outstretched to whatever lies ahead, I go straight for the goal—my reward the honor of being called by God in Christ" (Philippians 3:13, 14, PHILLIPS).

Stillness

Full moon on a silver sea, throwing into sharp relief the luminous rocks. I sat in the antique rocking chair by the window, a cup of hot Postum in my hand, fascinated by the undulation of great swaths of foam on the ocean, almost fluorescent in the moonlight.

Stillness. Perfect stillness. It is a very great gift, not always available to those who would most appreciate it and would find joy in it, and often not appreciated by those who have it but are uncomfortable with it. External noise is inescapable in many places—traffic on land and in the air, sirens, horns, chain saws, loud voices and, perhaps worst of all, screaming rock music with thundering amplification which makes the very ground shudder.

I think it is possible to *learn* stillness—but only if it is seriously sought. God tells us, "Be still, and know that I am God" (Psalm 46:10, NIV). "In quietness and confidence shall be your strength" (Isaiah 30:15, KJV).

The stillness in which we find God is not superficial, a mere absence of fidgeting or talking. It is a deliberate and quiet attentiveness—receptive, alert, ready. I think of what Jim Elliot wrote in his journal: "Wherever you are, be *all there*. Live to the hilt every situation you believe to be the will of God."

This is not so difficult, perhaps, for a sports fan, eyes riveted on the game. For me, however, this quietness in the presence of God, this being "all there" for Him, though I treasure it and long for it, is not easy to maintain, even in the beautiful place where I live. I am easily distracted, more so, it seems, as soon as I try to focus on God

Himself and nothing else. Why should this be? I think C.S. Lewis puts his finger right on it in *The Screwtape Letters*, which purports to be the correspondence between Screwtape, under-secretary to the devil, and his nephew, Wormwood, instructing him in the best ways to tempt the followers of the Enemy, God:

> My dear Wormwood: Music and silence—how I detest them both! How thankful we should be that ever since our Father entered Hell—though longer ago than humans, reckoning in light years, could express, no square inch of infernal space and no moment of infernal time has been surrendered to either of those abominable forces, but all has been occupied by Noise— Noise, the grand dynamism, the audible expression of all that is exultant, ruthless, and virile—Noise which alone defends us from silly qualms, despairing scruples, and impossible desires. We will make the whole universe a noise in the end. We have already made great strides in this direction as regards the Earth. The melodies and silences of Heaven will be shouted down in the end. But I admit we are not yet loud enough, or anything like it. Research is in progress.

C.S. Lewis died in 1963. Research in noise-making has made considerable progress since then, don't you think? To learn stillness we must resist our ancient foe, whose craft and power are great, and who is armed with cruel hate. There is One far greater who is on our side. His voice brought stillness to fierce winds and wild waves, and He will surely help us if we put ourselves firmly and determinedly in His presence—"I'm here, Lord. I'm listening." If no word seems to be forthcoming, remember "it is good to wait quietly for the salvation of the Lord," and "when He gives quietness, who then can make trouble?" (Lamentations 3:26, NIV; Job 34:29, KJV).

Silence is one form of worship. When the seventh seal was opened (in St. John's Revelation), there was silence in heaven for the space of half an hour. What would happen in our homes if we should try to prepare ourselves for those heavenly silences by having just one half-hour when there is no door slamming, no TV, no stereo or video, and a minimum of talk, in quiet voices? Wouldn't it also be a calming thing just to practice the stillness which is the absence of *motion*? My father used to have us try this every now and then. Why not try a Quiet Day or even a Quiet Week without the usual noises? It might open vistas of the spiritual life hitherto closed, a depth of communion with the Lord impossible where there is nothing but noise. Does God seem absent? Yes, for most of us He sometimes does. Even at such a time may we not simply be still before Him, trusting that He reads the perplexity we cannot put into words?

Section Three

Called and
Committed

If thou but suffer God to guide thee,
And hope in Him thro' all thy ways,
He'll give the strength, what-e'er betide thee,
And bear thee thro the evil days;
Who trust in God's unchanging love
Builds on the rock that naught can move.

Obey, thou restless heart, be still
And wait in cheerful hope, content
To take what-e'er His gracious will,
His all discerning love, hath sent;
Nor doubt our inmost wants are known
To Him who chose us for His own.

Sing, pray, and swerve not from His ways;
But do thine own part faithfully.
Trust His rich promises of grace,
So shall they be fulfilled in thee.
God never yet forsook in need
The soul that trusted Him indeed. Amen

Georg Neumark (Catherine Winkworth, Translator)
Inter-Varsity Hymnal

CRCED

Discerning the Call of God

As a little girl I especially loved the story of God's call to the child Samuel as he lay sleeping in the temple. I wondered if God would ever call me. Would I hear Him? What would He say? Throughout my growing years I read missionary stories and heard them told at our dinner table by guests from many lands who came to stay with us. I was always eager to know just how they were called. As a college student I worried much about whether I would fail to follow the Shepherd, would be deaf to His call. I thought it such a bewildering matter.

It is not a worry anymore. Experience has taught me that the Shepherd is far more willing to show His sheep the path than the sheep are to follow. He is endlessly merciful, patient, tender, and loving. If we, His stupid and wayward sheep, really want to be led, we will without fail be led. Of that I am sure.

When we need help, we wish we knew somebody who is wise enough to tell us what to do, reachable when we need him, and even able to help us. *God* is. Omniscient, omnipresent, omnipotent—everything we need. The issue is confidence in the Shepherd Himself, a confidence so complete that we offer ourselves without any reservation whatsoever and determine to do what He says.

What He *says*? But how shall I know that?

He calls us every day, "o'er the tumult of our life's wild, restless sea." He comes to us in the little things, in the ordinary duties which our place in life entails. When I was a child He called me.

The duty which my place in life entailed was obedience to my father and mother. In school and Sunday School He called me through the teacher. What she said I knew I was supposed to do. In first grade (yes, in public school) we sang the hymn, "Father, We Thank Thee." The second stanza says, "Help us to do the things we should, to be to others kind and good, in all we do at work or play to grow more loving every day." God's call again.

It's alluring to think of our own situation as very complex and ourselves as deep and complicated, so that we waste a good deal of time puzzling over "the will of God." Frequently our conscience has the answer.

My friend Jim O'Donnell tells how he, a hard-headed, hard-hearted man of the world, found Christ. His conscience was awakened. The call of God was immediate: "Go home and love your wife." The change was so sudden and so radical, Lizzie could not make head or tail of what had come over him. This self-confident and self-interested man had quit living for himself. He had *died*. An altogether new kind of life was now his. The first difference it made was the difference that mattered most—in his private life. It was there that he began to obey.

We are not talking here about audible voices. Although people in Bible times often heard God speak, we can expect that He will usually speak today through conscience, through the written Word, through other people, and through events. Events themselves, the seemingly insignificant happenings of every day, reveal the will of God. They *are* the will of God for us, for while we live, move, and have our being here on earth, in this place, this family, this house, this job, we live, move, and have our being *in God*. He "pulls strings through circumstances," as Jim Elliot said, even the bad circumstances (see Genesis 45:8, 50:20).

Three questions may help to clarify the call of God. Have I made up my mind to do what he says, no matter what the cost? Am I faithfully reading His Word and praying? Am I obedient in what I know today of His will?

"Let the morning bring me word of your unfailing love, for I have put my trust in you. Show me the way I should go, for to you I lift up my soul" (Psalm 143:8, NIV).

CRANO

How to Discover
What God Wants

A young woman came in great perplexity to a Scottish preacher, asking how she could resolve the question of her own desires when they seemed to be in such contradiction to the will of God. He took out a slip of paper, wrote two words on it, handed it to her with the request that she sit down for ten minutes, ponder the words, cross out one of them, and bring the slip back to him. She sat down and read: *No Lord.* Which to cross out? It did not take her long to see that if she was saying *No* she could not say *Lord,* and if she wanted to call Him *Lord,* she could not say *No.*

No question comes up more often among Christian young people who face what seem to be limitless options than this one of how to discover what God wants them to do. What, exactly, is one's calling?

There are two very simple conditions to discovering the will of God. Paul states them clearly in his letter to the Romans, chapter 12. The first is in verse 1 (Jerusalem Bible): "... offering your living bodies as a holy sacrifice, truly pleasing to God." The place to start is by putting yourself utterly and unconditionally at God's disposal. You say *Yes Lord.* You turn over all the rights at the very beginning. Once that's settled you can go on to the second, in verse 2: "Do not model yourselves on the behavior of the world around you, but let your behavior change, modelled by your new mind." I said that the conditions were simple. I did not say they were easy. Exchanging a *No Lord* for a *Yes Lord* has often been painful for me. But I do want a "new mind"—one that takes its cues from the Word of God, not the mass media. I pray for a clear eye to see through the fog of popular opinion, and a will strong enough to withstand the currents—a will surrendered, laid alongside Christ's. He is my model. This means a different set of ambitions, a different definition of happiness, a different standard of judgment altogether. Behavior will change, and very likely it will change enough to make me appear rather odd—but then my Master was thought very odd.

Paul goes on to say that these conditions are "the only way to discover the will of God and know what is good, what it is that God wants, what is the perfect thing to do." No wonder we scratch our heads and ask, "What *is* the secret of knowing the will of God?" We haven't started at the right place—the offering of that all-inclusive sacrifice, our very bodies, and then the resolute refusal of the world's values.

Make Thy paths known to me, O Lord; teach me Thy ways.
Lead me in Thy truth and teach me;
Thou art God my Savior.

Psalm 25:4, 5, NEB

When we cannot see our way
Let us trust and still obey;
He who bids us forward go
Cannot fail the way to show.
Though the sea be deep and wide,
Though a passage seem denied,
Fearless let us still proceed,
Since the Lord vouchsafes to lead.

Anonymous

If there is any man who fears the Lord, he shall be shown the path that he should choose.

Psalm 25:12, NEB

∞∞∞

Ungodly Counsel

"**B**lessed is the man that walketh not in the counsel of the ungodly" (Psalm 1:1, AV).

At a recent convention a young woman told me that her husband had wanted a divorce, but consented to see a Christian counselor before making it final. A member of the team in the counseling center told him that he himself was divorced and very happily remarried. That was all the husband needed. The man to whom he looked for help set the example he was hoping to find. Of course he went ahead and divorced his wife.

The twenty-third chapter of Jeremiah describes what is happening in our country today. The land is full of adulterers. Pastures have dried up. Powers are misused. Prophet and priest alike are godless, doing evil even in the Lord's house. Jeremiah's description of the prophets seems terribly fitting for some of those from whom Christian people are seeking guidance: "The vision they report springs from their own imagination. It is not from the mouth of the Lord.... To all who follow the promptings of their own stubborn heart they say, 'No disaster shall befall you.' But which of them has stood in the council of the Lord, seen him and heard his word? Which of them has listened to his word and obeyed?" (Jeremiah 23:16-18, NEB).

Here is a good test to apply to any of whom we seek counsel. Has this person stood in the council of the Lord? Seen Him? Heard His word? Listened and obeyed? Note the few who have actually paid a price for their obedience (like Jeremiah who was flogged, imprisoned, dropped into a pit of slime, etc.). These few are the ones to follow.

The chapter goes on to describe prophets who speak lies in God's name, dream dreams, give voice to their own inventions, concoct words of their own, and then say, "This is his very word." They mislead with "wild and reckless falsehoods."

"If a prophet has a dream, let him tell his dream; if he has my word, let him speak my word in truth. What has chaff to do with grain? says the Lord" (v. 28).

Beware of those who are afraid to quote Scripture, who say it's too "simplistic," doesn't apply here, won't work. Beware of the counselor who is "nondirectional." Be cautious when the advice given makes you feel comfortable when you know you're really wrong. "Do not my words scorch like fire? says the Lord. Are they not like a hammer that splinters rock?" (v. 29).

It wasn't only the awesome prophets of the Old Testament who spoke this way. Think of the words of Jesus. Though often He spoke "comfortable words," words that brought peace and hope, He spoke also those words that seared like fire ("Depart from me, I never knew you"; "Get behind me, Satan!") and splintered rock ("You will never get out until you have paid the last farthing"; "Whoever wants to be first must be the willing slave of all").

"The form of words you shall use in speaking amongst yourselves is: 'What answer has the Lord given?' or 'What has the Lord said?" (Jeremiah 23:35, NEB).

This applies, of course, only to those who care what the Lord wants. Those who have already decided to do their own thing need not apply for truly godly counsel.

∞∞∞

A Man Moves
Toward Marriage

L etters keep coming from both men and women who are in a quandary about how one ought to move toward marriage. While I was sitting here, rereading some of them, a man phoned with a question about the same subject. I wonder what is happening. Why so much confusion? Here's one of the letters:

"I'm a male Christian who needs help. I just ended a long-term 'relationship' with a non-Christian girl. I made plenty of compromises during those years, and by God's grace I hope next time will be better. I read your book *The Mark of a Man* and was shown things I never knew before which blew my mind. I'm excited about the idea of sharing life with a girl in a way which would honor Jesus. At the same time I get scared about making bad moves, when to initiate, and financial fears about supporting a family if I'm a missionary, which at the moment I'm being directed to. These things may seem silly but they're real to me. Could you address some issues which could benefit us guys who see marriage as a blessing and not as years of imprisonment?"

No, the questions do not seem silly to me—far from it. They are vital questions, and I'm glad there are men to whom they matter enough to pray about and ask counsel for.

I think one reason for confusion is the notion which arose, before the men who are now in their twenties and thirties were born, about the "equality" of the sexes. It is a word that belongs to politics but certainly not to courtship, a realm which concerns human beings in their entirety.

Another reason for confusion is misunderstanding the order which God established in the beginning. I've tried to explain that divine arrangement in two books: *Let Me Be a Woman* and *The Mark of a Man*. If men would be men, women could do a better job of being women (and *vice versa*, of course, but the buck really stops with the men). What does it mean to be a man?

Christ is the supreme example. He was strong and He was pure, because His sole aim in life was to be obedient to the Father. His very obedience made Him most manly—responsible, committed, courageous, courteous, and full of love. A Christian man's obedience to God will make him more of a man than anything else in the world. Consider these qualities:

Responsibility. He must work out the salvation that God has given him "with a proper sense of awe and responsibility, for it is God who is at work" in him, giving him the will and the power to achieve His purpose (Philippians 2:12, 13, PHILLIPS). Man was made to be initiator, provider, protector for woman.

Commitment. He must be a man of his word, no matter what it costs. My father's strong counsel to my four brothers: Never tell a woman you love her until you are ready to follow that immediately with, "Will you marry me?" In other words, a man's love for a woman, if deep and abiding, leads to a lifetime commitment to her. Many heartaches would be avoided if he held back any expressions of love until he is ready to make that commitment. Once promised, he never goes back on that word.

Courage. A man must be willing to take the risks of rejection (she might say No), blame, and all that commitment costs.

Courtesy. A Christian's rule of life should be, *My life for yours.* He is concerned about the comfort and happiness of others, not of himself. He does not seek to have his own needs met, his own image enhanced, but to love God, to make Him loved, and to lay down his life to that end. In small ways as well as great, he shows the courteous love of the Lord.

Purity. He must be master of himself if he is to be the servant of others. This means "buffeting" his body, bringing it into subjection, as Paul did. It means restraint, discipline, the strength to wait. It means an utter yielding to the will of God as revealed in 1 Corinthians 6:12-20 and 1 Thessalonians 4:2-8.

As I have heard the sad stories and studied what I call "The Dating Mess" of today, it appears to me that men have generally overlooked another vital matter which ought to *precede* all overtures in the direction of a prospective wife. If we assume that a man is an adult when he is eighteen (or twenty-one at the latest), he should by that time be giving marriage some serious thought. He should get down to brass tacks with God to find out if this may be a part of His agenda for him. This will take time, and it might help if during this period he simply quits dating and starts praying. As long as the answer is uncertain, don't date. Does this sound extreme? It wasn't my idea. I learned it from a group of young men who have chosen this way. It is a guaranteed way of avoiding sexual activity (always illicit outside of marriage), of preserving one's wholeness and holiness, and of preventing the heartbreaks we see on every hand.

I urge you to trust God. He wants to give you the best. He will help you. He has promised to guide. He knows what you need. Ask Him to show you *whether, when,* and *whom* you should marry.

And don't be alone in this. Ask counsel of your spiritual superiors who are wise, who know how to pray and how to keep silence. Take their counsel seriously. If they have suggestions as to a possible mate, take those very seriously. My own parents prayed for godly spouses for all six of us, and actually named before God the very people that four of us married.

Read Genesis 24, study the principles Abraham's servant followed. Pray silently. Watch quietly.

Before you start dating, draw clear guidelines for yourself as to "how far to go." The only truly safe line is a radical one, but *it works:* hands off and clothes on. If you think you can put the line somewhere else, remember that a little thing leads on to a bigger thing. A touch leads to a hug which leads to a kiss which leads to play which leads to consummation. That was how God intended the whole thing to work, but the idea of the "whole thing" was marriage and babies.

Can you trust yourself to quit once you start? The Bible says, "Flee youthful lusts." Don't toy with them.

When God has guided you* as to the whether, the when, and the whom, then you must choose to love and not to fear. The Will of God always involves risk and cost, but He is there with grace to help and with all the wisdom you need. Every deliberate choice to obey Him will—depend upon it—be attacked by the enemy. Never mind. Nothing new about that. Be a man and stick with it.

* My little book *A Slow and Certain Light* deals with the question of how to discern the Lord's will.

CRASCRO

Virginity

M y heart goes out to the countless women in their thirties and forties who write to me in real agony of soul because they are still single. Here are two letters. One says, "I am a Christian woman thirty years of age and I am facing the possibility of a life of singleness." The other: "I am forty-one years old. I never dreamed I would not be married—I've been praying for a husband ever since I was sixteen."

This phenomenon is due in part, I suppose, to what demographers are calling "the postponed generation" (the Baby Boomers, born between 1946 and 1964) which has reached catastrophic proportions. Men postpone marriage ten or twenty years beyond what used to be considered the marrying age. When the mirror tells them they're fast aging they decide it's time to settle down. Feeling that a young wife will lend a certain assurance that they are not quite over the hill, they pass up women of their own age. Everywhere my husband and I go we meet lovely Christian women, beautifully dressed, deeply spiritual, thoroughly feminine—and *single*. They long for marriage and children. But what is it with the men? Are they blind to feminine pulchritude, deaf to God's call, numb to natural desire?

I am reminded of the conversation I had with Gladys Aylward thirty years ago. She had been a missionary in China for six or seven years before she ever thought of wanting a husband. When a British couple came to work near her she began to watch the wonderful thing they had in marriage, and to desire it for herself. Being a woman of prayer she prayed—a straightforward request that God would call a man from England, send him straight out to China, and have him propose. She leaned toward me on the sofa on which we were sitting, her black eyes snapping, her bony little forefinger jabbing at my face. "Elisabeth," she said, "I *believe* God answers prayer! He *called* him," then, in a whisper of keen intensity, "but he *never came.*"

Where are the holy men of God willing to shoulder the full responsibility of manhood, to take the risks and make the sacrifices of courting and winning a wife, marrying her and fathering children in obedience to the command to be fruitful? While the Church has been blessed by men willing to remain single *for the sake of the Kingdom* (and I do not regard lightly such men who are seriously called), isn't it obvious that God calls most men to marriage? By not marrying, those whom He calls are disobeying Him, and thus are denying the women He meant for them to marry the privileges of being wife and mother.

But what shall I say to the women who write to me in such sorrow and perplexity? First of all, it is not our job to set about trying to coerce the men. They must answer to God who made *them* the initiators. But a woman must answer to God by her acceptance of singleness, seeking to know Him in it and converting it into good by a peaceful *Yes, Lord!* rather than into real evil by a rebellious *No!*

Lars says, "I'll tell you what would change things fast—if *all* women decided they would not 'give out,' I mean give men what they're looking for but are unwilling to make a commitment for."

One young woman wrote in desperation, agreeing with what I believe is God's order, "YEAH! That's the way it should be!! Unfortunately, that's not the way it *is!*"

God's order is not changed by men's (or women's) disobedience. It stands as He ordained. In the long run we gain nothing and lose much if we take things into our own hands. A woman may "gain" a husband, of course. The more obvious she makes herself, the better her chances seem to be in today's society. But a man who is attracted to such a woman, and a woman who is out to "get" men, are not submissive to God's order, it seems to me. Let's not follow that pattern. To follow His is to lose nothing, in the long run, and to gain much— "lose your *life*," as Jesus put it, "for My sake, and you'll find it." Few seem to believe that enough to stake their all on it.

Is there a formula which will "work"? I am asked. My parents' formula "worked" for me: they prayed for spouses for us six; they taught us to pray and trust God. Mother told me, "Keep them at arm's length, don't chase them." This will not "work" in the sense of providing a surefire method of snaring a husband (I never *snared* any one of the three God has given me—He brought them to me in most astonishing and unlikely ways). But it is in keeping with a Christian woman's modesty and willingness to have what God wants for her. She is not putting hooks out, but rather doing quietly the work God has given her to do, confident that His promise can be trusted: "No good thing will he withhold from them that walk uprightly" (Psalm 84:11, KJV). If marriage is a good thing for *you*, God will see to it that you receive that gift. Only He knows whether it is good for *you*. Are you willing to be and have what He wants you to be and have, and nothing else? Will you surrender all your own hopes, dreams, and plans to Him?

"That's easy for you to say," some answer. "Look what God has given you." Yes, but I did not know that He would ever give me a husband when I gave Him my hopes, dreams, and plans. I *did not know*. I had to surrender to Him, believing that whatever He gave or did not give would be *best*.

Friends offer all sorts of advice to single women: don't be too aggressive or too backward, too friendly or too hard-to-get, too intellectual or too dumb, too earthy or too heavenly. Hang around till the bitter end of the singles barbecue—he might want to take you home. Or, don't go to the singles barbecue at all. Just stay home and read your Bible and pray. It's terribly confusing.

"Is my Father in charge here or am I supposed to take over?" He is in charge if you want Him to be. He will not invade your freedom to choose to "take over." But if you want His way, nothing more, nothing less, and nothing *else*, you've got to leave it to Him. It's easy to be deceived here—telling ourselves we really want His will, but meaning "I want it so long as it includes marriage!"

"I don't know how to play the game," wrote one frustrated girl. Nobody does. It's chaos, frustration, confusion, and emotional devastation. It was never meant to be a game, so don't try to play it. Leave it all in the Hands that were wounded for you.

Another who was trying to take the burden onto her own slim shoulders said it was making her "just plain sick." I do not wonder at that. She is taking burdens He never meant her to bear. "Come to Me," He says, "all of you who are weary and overburdened, and I will give you rest. Take My yoke upon you and learn from Me, for I am gentle and humble in heart" (Matthew 11:28-29, PHILLIPS). It's all a question of utter surrender in love for God above all others. "Everything that happens fits into a pattern for good" to them that love God, Romans 8:28 tells us (PHILLIPS). Loving God means a final and unreserved YES to all of His holy will, and if His holy will is singleness, that too fits the pattern and the pattern is good.

"How can a Christian single woman enter into the mystery of Christ and the Church if she never experiences marriage?" is the question of a very thoughtful young woman.

The gift of virginity, given to everyone to offer back to God for His use, is a priceless and irreplaceable gift. It can be offered in the pure sacrifice of marriage, or it can be offered in the sacrifice of a life's celibacy. Does this sound just too, too high and holy? But think for a moment—because the virgin has never known a man, she is free to concern herself wholly with the Lord's affairs, as Paul said in 1 Corinthians 7, "and her aim in life is to make herself holy, in body and spirit" (PHILLIPS). She keeps her heart as the Bride of Christ in a very special sense, and offers to the Heavenly Bridegroom alone all that she is and has. When she gives herself willingly to Him in love, she has no need to justify herself to the world or to Christians who plague her with questions and suggestions. In a way not open to the married woman her daily "living sacrifice" is a powerful and humble witness, radiating love. I believe she may enter into the "mystery" more deeply than the rest of us.

"How can she enter into the mystery of the Father loving His children if she never has children?" But she *can* have children! She may be a spiritual mother, as was Amy Carmichael, by the very offering of her singleness, transformed for the good of far more children than a natural mother may produce. All is received and made holy by the One to whom it is offered.

There. I've lengthened this chapter for this subject, but my correspondence files tell me it is a pressing subject indeed, and I do long to help in any way I can those who find no help or comfort or support whatsoever from the world, and, alas, precious little sometimes from the Church itself.

"If you had been of the world," said our Savior, "the world would love its own; but because you are not of the world, but I have chosen you out of the world, therefore the world hateth you" (John 15:19, KJV). Remember this, too—"The world and all its passionate desires will one day disappear. But the [one] who is following God's will is part of the permanent and cannot die" (1 John 2:17, PHILLIPS).

∞∞

Self-Pity

A single woman missionary writes, "I've never dated anyone. Is it realistic for a woman to desire confirmation of her femininity at one point in her life? Do I have cause to feel sorry for myself? To be mad at God for leaving me in such dire social straits? I already know the answer, of course! I'm like the children of Israel demanding of Samuel, 'We want a king such as all the other nations have.' Here I am with the greatest of Bridegrooms, complaining because I'm physically lonely and want to be like other women.... I long to know what it's like to be loved by a man. The thought of a life without ever experiencing it makes me so very sad and all the more aware that I have a long way to go before I'll ever be the kind of woman *God* wants me to be."

To the first question I would answer yes, it's realistic, it's natural, it's not wrong. A real woman's desire is to be a real woman, and a man's love helps to confirm that. But human desire is to be brought under the lordship of Christ for fulfillment according to *His* wisdom and choosing. (See Psalm 10:17; 37:4; 38:9; 145:19.)

"He gives the very best to those who leave the choice with Him."

To the second and third questions I would say no, as my correspondent guessed. We are never warranted in feeling sorry for ourselves or being "mad" at God—He loves us with an Everlasting Love; He died for us; His will is always love and, when we accept it in loving trust, it is our *peace*.

Another letter came just a couple of weeks after the above, also from a single woman missionary. "I appreciate very much the honesty and openness with which you talk about missionary life, and the importance you place on obedience and leaving the results in God's hands. That has helped me to know the cost, and to know and give credit to the One who makes any success here possible.... Being obedient to Him *is* good! Obedience gives an incredible peace, and every now and then I think God allows us a glimpse of how He's working out His plan here, and it's awesome! You're right—obedience is worth the cost!"

∽∞∾

The Childless Man
or Woman

Children, God tells us, are a heritage from Him. Is the man or woman to whom he gives no children therefore disinherited? Surely not. The Lord gave portions of land to each tribe of Israel except one. "The tribe of Levi... received no holding; the Lord God of Israel is their portion, as he promised them" (Joshua 13:14, NEB). Withholding what He granted to the rest, He gave to Levi a higher privilege. May we not see childlessness in the same light? I believe there is a special gift for those to whom God does not give the gift of physical fatherhood or motherhood.

I have known many women (and a few men) who have sorrowed deeply over being childless. My brother-in-law Bert Elliot and his wife Colleen, missionaries in Peru for more than forty years, longed for children of their own. They asked the Lord for children if that would best glorify Him. His answer was no. They wondered about adoption, which would not have been nearly so difficult there as it is in the States. Again the answer seemed to be no, but God has given them the privilege of fathering and mothering hundreds of Peruvians, both white and Indian, in the jungle and in the high Andes, where they bear on their shoulders the care of dozens of little churches.

A woman of about fifty wrote, "Each Mother's Day became a little harder for me as I realized another year had gone by and after many years of marriage I am still childless—the only woman in my Sunday School class who is not a mother. The morning service started... I could not see the pastor for the tears in my eyes. Almost at the end of his message he said, 'I know there are some of you women here this morning who would like to be mothers, but for some reason God has chosen differently. Don't question Him. He has a reason.'"

Childlessness, for those who deeply desire children, is real suffering. Seen in the light of Calvary and accepted in the name of Christ, it becomes a chance to share in His sufferings. Acceptance of the will of the Father took Him to the Cross. We find our peace as we identify with Him in His death and resurrection.

Look around your church. If you are a parent, look for those who aren't. Might they not be ready to "father" or "mother" you or your children, to be adopted as a grandparent, for example, or an aunt or uncle? My life was enriched by unmarried aunts and friends who paid attention to us children, celebrated our birthdays and sometimes even helped us with homework. The love they would have poured out on their own children had God given them marriage, they poured out instead on us, and we were blessed as we could not have been had they had children. Their loss was our gain, and, as Ugo Bassi, a young Italian preacher, said many years ago, we are to measure our lives "by loss and not by gain, not by the wine drunk but by the wine poured forth, for Love's strength standeth in Love's sacrifice, and he who suffereth most hath most to give."

What of the thousands who have not had the mothers and fathers they desperately longed for while they were growing up? Is not God calling all whose ears are open to Him to recognize the wounds of the world and to pour forth His love to the lonely young man whose relationship with his father seems to have destroyed his fitness for manhood? Or to the expectant mother whose own mother is far away, or indifferent, or dead, who longs for a mother to share her joy? Whose will be the strong shoulder of sympathy (the word means "to suffer *with*") ready to bear another's burdens?—not with the tepid sentimentality which only weakens, but with the burning love which gives hope and cheer and strength?

My correspondent says God has given her "several kids adopted in my heart to pray for, whose mothers say they haven't time to pray." Another girl asked her to be grandmother to her new baby. "Well, what a blessing and how this has changed my life!" she says. "If I had sat around and felt sorry for myself look at the above blessings I would have missed. What a thrill on Mother's Day this year to get a Grandmother card!"

And what of the young childless woman? Is she merely to mark time, hoping against hope that someday she will be given a child? There are always younger people who need a boost, some encouragement in their struggles against the pull of the world, a listening ear when they face hard decisions, someone who will simply take time out to pray with them, to walk with them the way of the cross with its tremendous demand—the difficult and powerful life of glad surrender and acceptance. As the branches of the wine pour out their sweetness, so young women may see their opportunity, as branches of the True Vine, to pour out their lives for the world.

∽∾∽

Church Troubles

When the church prays "hallowed be thy name" it is usually pretty obvious that that holy name is far from hallowed in the way we as church members behave. In our travels we see and hear much about church troubles, and I am always reminded of the high priestly prayer of the Lord Jesus just before He went to the cross. As He prayed for believers ("those you have given me") His petition was, "Holy Father, protect them by the power of your name—the name you gave me—so that they may be one as we are one" (John 17:11, NIV). For those who would later believe He prayed, "that all of them may be one, Father.... May they be brought to complete unity to let the world know that you sent me and have loved them even as you have loved me" (John 17:21; 23, NIV).

The answer to that prayer seems yet remote. Ought we not to put ourselves, each of us as individuals, in a position to cooperate with God in His bringing about this unity? How shall the world recognize His love unless we act in love toward one another? No one, I feel sure, would disagree here—in theory. *Love each other.* The obstacle is our selfish, self-determined selves.

Most churches have problems with the choir. Martin Luther said, "If you can confine the devil's work to the choir, do so." But let's suppose that the problem seems to be the pastor. (I confess to a certain bias in favor of these harried souls—I have a nephew, two-nephews-in-law, a son-in-law, and a brother who are pastors). He's too young or too old, too conservative or too liberal, his sermons are irrelevant to our needs, or too long or too pointed for this congregation, he's a social mismatch, not sensitive to the variety of folks we've got here, he's partial—in short, we got the wrong man, it's a bad mix, the solution is simple: get rid of him. Then all will be well.

Before we take such a position of sovereignty, assuming we *know* the root of the trouble and are warranted in enforcing our "solution," might we not ask ourselves a few questions? (I do *not* refer here, of course, to cases which unequivocally call for dismissal, such as immorality or heresy.)

1. Who called this pastor? Was it the bishop? The church? Was the decision prayed over? Do we believe in the Holy Spirit's guidance?

2. Do we understand the shepherd of the flock to be one who bears responsibility and authority? "Encourage and rebuke with all authority" was the apostle Paul's word to a young shepherd (Titus 2:15, NIV). To Timothy he said, "Command and teach" (1 Timothy 4:11, NIV). "Obey your leaders and submit to their authority... so that their work will be a joy, not a burden" (Hebrews 13:17, NIV). Have we respected that divine assignment?

3. If the sheep send the shepherd out of the fold, will not the sheep themselves be devastated, as well as the shepherd? Spiritual devastation is often the result of taking things into our own hands. No humility is wrought in us, no more robust faith is born.

4. Have we learned the meekness which understands the power of patience, of quiet waiting on God, and the futility of employing massive methods to get our own way? What about the reverence that trusts God's hidden, seemingly slow, working out of His own mysterious purposes? Impatience hardens.

5. Have we challenged evil with the wrong weapons? "By the meekness and gentleness of Christ, I appeal to you.... Though we live in the world, we do not wage war as the world does. The weapons we fight with are not the weapons of the world. On the contrary, they have divine power to demolish strongholds" (2 Corinthians 10:1,3-4, NIV).

6. Are we willing to accept suffering? How much do we know of costly action, sacrificial love? Have we been willing to lay down our lives for this man, travail in prayer, accept the cross in the depths of our own hearts? The demands of faith cut across human logic and politics, and often oppose all ordinary methods and even common sense.

7. Have we pondered Jesus' warning not to expect His church to be without spot or wrinkle? The net brings in good fish and bad. The tares grow along with the wheat. He is at work perfecting His own bride—we'll never manage it ourselves.

8. Are we willing to let the cross cut painfully—humbly to relinquish our grasp of what we believe to be the true nature of the conflict, let go of our certainties of what "ought to be," and of our particular "rights"? Can we, in the spirit of Christ, mortify our whims, accept setbacks, accustom ourselves to misunderstanding, quit asking "What about *my* needs?" Let God take care of those—He promised He would, *all* of them.

"The Christian turns again and again from that bewildered contemplation of history in which God is so easily lost, to the prayer of filial trust in which He is always found, knowing here that those very things which seem to turn to man's disadvantage may yet work to the Divine advantage. On the frontier between prayer and history stands the Cross, a perpetual reminder of the price by which the Kingdom is brought in" (Evelyn Underhill, *Abba*).

Perhaps, if we would earnestly and prayerfully consider these things, both pastor and flock might be changed and the severance thus avoided. Perhaps not, but in the process we, the sheep, will certainly have learned to trust the Chief Shepherd more fully, and will have become a little more like Him.

> Love divine has seen and counted
> Every tear it caused to fall,
> And the storm which Love appointed
> Was its choicest gift of all.

Anonymous

∞∞∞

My Spiritual Mother

Katherine Morgan has been a missionary in Pasto, Colombia, for more than fifty years. She has been a friend of mine for more than forty-three of those years and has done for me what Paul said Onesiphorus did for him: refreshed me often. Katherine's husband died when they had been married only six years, but she carried on their missionary work and reared their four little girls. To Katherine I owe more than I can ever tell. She more or less booted me to Ecuador. I was a missionary candidate without a field, didn't know quite how to find one, talked to her, and within months found myself in Quito. She had had me in her home many weekends, giving me previews of coming attractions—what not to expect from "supporters," what to expect from them, what to expect from Ecuadorians and from jungle Indians, what to take (a sense of humor, for one thing), what not to take (a sense of smell, a trunkful of inhibitions and Plymouth Brethren prejudices, an inflated idea of my own importance, and the notion that people are longing to hear the gospel). At times all of us—her daughters were in junior high and high school then—would be nearly rolling on the floor with laughter. One evening we had a hat show. Katherine had come home from a missionary meeting with a shopping bag full of hats that a lady told her the Lord had "laid on my heart to give to the missionaries."

A few years ago she called me from Pennsylvania where she was visiting a daughter. She just wanted to chat while it would still be easy to chat, since she'd be going back to Colombia in a few weeks. Asking about a mutual friend who had been in the hospital, she told me to tell her to jump up and praise the Lord. She mentioned a gift sent to her which had been designated for a retired missionary. "Me—retired! I haven't even thought of retiring." She sent it back. We talked about "travailing," for people who have fallen away from the Lord. I reminded her of 2 Corinthians 4, the passage about bearing "death in our bodies" in order that life may work in others. Yes, she agreed, that's in the Bible, all right, but she couldn't think of herself in that way—"I'm too cheerful"—even though I happen to know she has suffered many kinds of death for the sake of other people (and has had her own life threatened a number of times, including being stoned and doused with gasoline more than once).

Dear Katherine! "A merry heart doeth good like a medicine." Hers has been an elixir for me. She's one of those who bring forth fruit in old age—though she'd hit me for suggesting she's anywhere near that category. May God make me like her.

∽∽∽

A Call to Older Women

In 1948 when I had been at Prairie Bible Institute (a very stark set of wooden buildings on a very bleak prairie in Alberta) for only a few weeks, I was feeling a bit displaced and lonesome one afternoon when there came a knock on my door. I opened it to find a beautiful rosy-cheeked face framed by white hair. She spoke with a charming Scottish burr.

"You don't know me, but I know you. I've been prraying forr you, Betty dearr. I'm Mrs. Cunningham. If everr you'd like a cup of tea and a Scottish scone, just pop down to my little aparrtment."

She told me where she lived and went on to say that my name had been mentioned in a staff meeting (she never said how—was I thought of as a misfit at PBI? I wonder) and the Lord had given her a burden for me. Many were the wintry afternoons when I availed myself of her gracious offer and we sat together in her tiny but very cozy basement apartment while she poured tea for me and I poured my soul out to her. Her radiant face was full of sympathy, love, and understanding as she listened. She would be quiet for a little, then she would pray and, looking up, cheer and strengthen me with words from God. During and after my missionary years she wrote to me until she died. Only God knows what I owe to "the four Katharines"—Katharine Cunningham, Katharine Gillingham Howard (my own mother), Katherine Cumming (my house mother when I was in college), and Katherine Morgan. These and several others have not only shown me what godliness looks like (many have done that), but have significantly graced my life by obeying God's special call to older women.

The apostle Paul tells Titus that older women ought to "school the younger women to be loving wives and mothers, temperate, chaste, and kind, busy at home, respecting the authority of their own husbands" (Titus 2:4-5, NEB). My dear "Mom Cunningham" schooled me—not in a class or seminar, or even primarily by her words. It was what she *was* that taught me. It was her availability to God when He sent her to my door. It was the surrender of her *time*, an offering to Him for my sake. It was her readiness to "get involved," to lay down her life for one anxious Bible school girl. Above all, she herself, a simple Scottish woman, *was the message*.

I think of the vast number of older women today. The Statistical Abstract of the United States for 1980 says that 19.5 percent of the population was between ages 45-65, but by 2000 it will be 22.9 percent. Assuming that half of those people are women, what a pool of energy and power for God they might be. We live longer now than we did forty years ago (the same volume says that the over-sixty-fives will increase from 11.3 percent to 13 percent). There is more mobility, more money around, more leisure, more health and strength—resources which, if put at God's disposal, might bless younger women. But there are also many more ways to *spend* those resources, so we find it very easy to occupy ourselves selfishly. Where are the women, single or married, willing to hear God's call to spiritual motherhood, taking spiritual daughters under their wings to school them as Mom Cunningham did me? She had no training the world would recognize. She had no thought of such. She simply loved God and was willing to be broken bread and poured-out wine for His sake. *Retirement* never crossed her mind.

If some of my readers are willing to hear this call but hardly know how to begin, may I suggest to you:

1. Pray about it. Ask God to show you whom, what, how.

2. Consider writing notes to or telephoning some younger woman who needs encouragement in the areas Paul mentioned.

3. Ask a young mother if you may do her ironing, take the children out, babysit so she can go out, make a cake or a casserole for her.

4. Do what Mom C. did for me—invite somebody to tea, find out

what she'd like you to pray for (I asked her to pray that God would bring Jim Elliot and me together!)—and *pray* with her.

5. Start a little prayer group of two or three whom you can cheer and help. You'll be cheered and helped too!

6. Organize a volunteer housecleaning pool to go out every other week or once a month to somebody who needs you.

7. Have a lending library of books of real spiritual food.

8. Be the first of a group in your church to be known as the WOTT's (Women of Titus Two), and see what happens (something will).

"Say not you cannot gladden, elevate, and set free; that you have nothing of the grace of influence; that all you have to give is at the most only common bread and water. Give yourself to your Lord for the service of men with what you have. Cannot He change water into wine? Cannot He make stammering words to be instinct [imbued, filled, charged] with saving power? Cannot He change trembling efforts to help into deeds of strength? Cannot He still, as of old, enable you in all your personal poverty 'to make many rich?' God has need of thee for the service of thy fellow men. He has a work for thee to do. To find out what it is, and then to do it, is at once thy supremist duty and thy highest wisdom. 'Whatsoever He saith unto you, do it.'" (Canon George Body, b. 1840)

CRITICAL

Starting a WOTTS Group

Men and women who are committed to obedience to Titus 2:1-5 are desperately needed in the world, in the church, and in the home. Writing on what I called spiritual motherhood I referred to them as WOTTs (Women of Titus Two). A reader asks if I have guidelines, structure, organization, information about such a group. Well, not much—for this reason: as soon as you organize, you have to have meetings! What we don't need is one more meeting to take us away from our homes and telephones. My suggestions are simply these:

1. Pray. Ask God to show you the needs and ways in which you yourself can help. Pray (perhaps on the phone if it's difficult to get together) with one or two others who understand the need.

2. Ask your pastor if he might preach on the Titus passage. It will take courage for him to do this.

3. In Bible studies, Sunday School classes, over your kitchen table or wherever you have opportunity, raise the subject of spiritual motherhood. Tell others of the blessing your own spiritual mothers have been to you. (If you had none, find a model in a book, as I did in missionary author Amy Carmichael. Then seek to be one.)

4. Post a list on the church bulletin board of the WOTTs, women who earnestly desire to be available. Mothers (in the usual sense and in the spiritual) are people who must be available—not all the time, not to meet every demand, but as needs arise which

they can meet. They are prepared to do so, no matter how humble and unsung the job. The deepest needs are for godly examples, ears to hear, shoulders to cry on, hearts to pray. Then there are the humble tasks which lighten others' burdens: drive someone to the doctor, do somebody's ironing, take a friend and go clean somebody's refrigerator and oven (jobs young mothers find it hard to get around to); babysit—in your house or theirs. Rock a baby, read a story, cook the supper, do the mending. Take an old person shopping and to lunch. Clean the house, do the gardening, write letters at his or her dictation or acquire some government postcards—so cheap, so easy to write a note on if *you* address them first.

God will give you many other ideas if you ask Him.

∞∞∞

Women of Like Passions

The leader of a women's conference asked me if I would be able to talk privately with a young woman who was in deep sorrow. This woman didn't want to "bother" me, the leader said, didn't feel she ought to take my time when there were hundreds of others who needed it. In fact, she was scared of me. Of course I said I'd be very glad to talk with her, and please to tell her I was not fierce.

After the talk, the young woman went to report to the leader.

"Oh, it wasn't bad after all! I walked in—I was shaking. I looked into her eyes, and I knew that she, too, had suffered. Then she gave me this beautiful smile. When I saw that huge space between her front teeth, I said to myself, 'it's OK—she's not perfect!'"

My daughter Valerie once taught a women's Bible class in Laurel, Mississippi. It happened that she lost her place in her notes as she was speaking. She tried to find it while continuing to speak, realized she couldn't, apologized and paused to search the page. The pause grew agonizingly long. At last she gave up and ad-libbed through the rest of the lesson. She couldn't find the application, couldn't find the conclusion. Leaving the platform afterwards, she was on the point of tears because of what seemed an abysmal failure. A lady came to her to say it was the best class so far. Later someone called to thank Val for things which had helped her.

"Mama," she told me on the phone, "I couldn't understand why this had happened. I had prepared faithfully, done the best I could. But then I remembered a prayer I'd prayed that week (Walt told me it was a ridiculous prayer!)—asking the Lord to make those women know that I'm just an ordinary woman like the rest of them and I need His help. I guess this was His answer, don't you think?"

Calmly we look behind us, on joys
and sorrows past,
We know that all is mercy now,
and shall be well at last;
Calmly we look before us,—
we fear no future ill,
Enough for safety and for peace,
if Thou art with us still.

Jane Borthwick

∞∞∞

Nothing Is Lost

A pastor's wife asked, "When one witnesses a work he has poured his life into 'go up in flames' (especially if he is not culpable), is it the work of Satan or the hand of God?"

Often it is the former, always it is under the control of the latter. In the biographies of the Bible we find men whose work for God seemed to be a flop at the time—Moses' repeated efforts to persuade Pharaoh, Jeremiah's pleas for repentance, the good king Josiah's reforms, rewarded in the end by his being slain by a pagan king. Sin had plenty to do with the seeming failures, but God was then, as He is now, the "blessed controller of all things" (1 Timothy 6:15, PHILLIPS). He has granted to us human beings responsibility to make choices and to live with the consequences. This means that everybody suffers—sometimes for his or her own sins, sometimes for those of others.

There are paradoxes here which we cannot plumb. But we can always look at the experiences of our own lives in the light of the life of our Lord Jesus. How shall we learn to "abide" (stay put) in Christ, enter into the fellowship of His sufferings, let Him transform our own? There is only one way. It is by living each event, including having things "go up in flames," as Christ lived: in the peace of the Father's will. Did His earthly work appear to be a thundering success? He met with argument, unbelief, scorn in Pharisees and others. Crowds followed Him—not because they wanted His Truth, but because they liked handouts such as bread and fish and physical healing. His own disciples were "fools and slow of heart to believe." (Why didn't Jesus *make* them believe? For the reason given above.) These men who had lived intimately with Him, heard

His teaching for three years, watched His life and miracles, still had little idea what He was talking about on the evening before His death. Judas betrayed Him, Peter denied Him. The rest of them went to sleep when He asked them to stay awake. In the end they all forsook Him and fled. Peter repented with tears and later saw clearly what had taken place. In his sermon to the Jews of Jerusalem (Acts 2:23, PHILLIPS) he said, "This man, who was put into your power by the predetermined plan and foreknowledge of God, you nailed up and murdered.... But God would not allow the bitter pains of death to touch him. He raised him to life again—and there was nothing by which death could hold such a man."

There is nothing by which death can hold any of His faithful servants, either. Settle it, once and for all—YOU CAN NEVER LOSE WHAT YOU HAVE OFFERED TO CHRIST. It's the man who tries to save himself (or his reputation or his work or his dreams of success or fulfillment) who loses. Jesus gave us His word that if we'd lose our lives for His sake, we'd find them.

∽∾∽

The Unseen Company

Many of us belong to churches where a creed is often repeated by the congregation. Several of the ancient creeds include these words, "I believe in the communion of saints." For some the word *saints* means only certain specially holy people who have been officially designated as such. For others it means those who are now in heaven. The Bible is very matter-of-fact in showing that those who belong to Christ, i.e., Christians, are saints. Look at Acts 9:32 and 41 for a start. Then note the salutations in Romans 1:7, 1 Corinthians 1:2, and other places.

Do you ever think much about that communion? Do you actually believe in it? I'm learning. The *communion* of saints takes no notice of location. Here or on the other side of the world or in heaven, all who love the Lord are included, bound together as a body whose Head is Christ. The gallery of heroes of the faith in Hebrews 11 comprises not only those who achieved thrilling victories through faith, but also the destitute and persecuted, those who were tortured, flogged, imprisoned, and even sawn in two—people whom the world would never deem worthy, yet the Bible says the world was not worthy of *them!* And here's something worth pausing over: *all* were "commended for their faith, yet *none* of them received what had been promised. God had planned something better for us, so that only together with us would they be made perfect" (vv. 39-40).

When I pray I am often preoccupied and distracted, aware that my efforts are feeble and seemingly quite useless, but the thought that those distinguished heroes are to be perfected along with me (and with the writer of Hebrews, and with you and all the rest of the followers of the Lamb) changes the picture altogether and puts new heart into me. Grand and mysterious things are in operation. We are not alone. My prayers are perhaps a single note in a symphony, but a necessary note, for I believe in the communion of saints. We need each other. The prayers of one affect all. The obedience of one matters infinitely and forever.

We are told that we are "surrounded by a great cloud of witnesses" (Hebrews 12:1, KJV)—those who found in Christ "their Rock, their Fortress, and their Might, their Captain in the well-fought fight" (to borrow the words of an old hymn), and "in the darkness drear their one true Light—Alleluia" (W.W. How: "For All the Saints").

When newly married and living in a little palm-thatched house in the jungle, Jim Elliot and I remembered that even in so remote a place we were still gathered in that great communion, and we used often to sing John Ellerton's hymn, "The Day Thou Gavest, Lord, Is Ended." (Lars and I sometimes sing it now.) My favorite stanzas:

We thank Thee that Thy Church, unsleeping,
While earth rolls onward into light,
Through all the world her watch is keeping,
And rests not now by day or night.

As o'er each continent and island
The dawn brings on another day,
The voice of prayer is never silent,
Nor die the strains of praise away.

Maybe there is a reader who is very weak and very lonely as he reads this today, tempted to feel that prayer is futile and goes nowhere. Think of the great Unseen Company that watches and prays as we "run with perseverance the race marked out for us" (Hebrews 12:1, NIV)! Think of that and be of good cheer—it's much too soon to quit!

∞∞∞

The World Must Be Shown

W hen Jesus was speaking with His disciples before His cruci-fixion, He gave them His parting gift: peace such as the world can never give. But He went on immediately to say, "Set your trou-bled hearts at rest and banish your fears.... I shall not talk much longer with you, for the Prince of this world approaches. He has no rights over me, but the world must be shown that I love the Father and do exactly as He commands" (John 14:27, 30-31, NEB).

A young mother called to ask for "something that will help me to trust in the Lord." She explained that she had several small chil-dren, she herself was thirty years old, and she had cancer. Chemotherapy had done its hideous work of making her totally bald. The prognosis was not good. Could I say to her, "Set your troubled heart at rest. God is going to heal you"? Certainly not. Jesus did not tell His disciples that He would not be killed. How do I know whether God would heal this young woman? I could, how-ever, remind her that He would not for a moment let go of her, that His love enfolded her and her precious children every minute of every day and every night, and that underneath are the Everlasting Arms.

But is that enough? The terrible things in the world seem to make a mockery of the love of God, and the question always arises: *Why?*

There are important clues in the words of Jesus. The disciples' worst fears were about to be realized, yet He commanded (yes, *commanded*) them to be at peace. All would be well, all manner of things would be well—in the end. In a short time, however, the Prince of this world, Satan himself, was to be permitted to have his way. Not that Satan had any rights over Jesus. Far from it. Nor has he "rights" over any of God's children, including that dear mother. But Satan is permitted to approach. He challenges God, we know from the Book of Job, as to the validity of His children's faith.

God allows him to make a test case from time to time. It had to be proved to Satan, in Job's case, that there is such a thing as obedient faith which does not depend on receiving only benefits. Jesus had to show the world that He loved the Father and would, no matter what happened, do exactly what He said. The servant is not greater than his Lord. When we cry "Why, Lord?" we should ask instead, "Why not, Lord? Shall I not follow my Master in suffering as in everything else?"

Does our faith depend on having every prayer answered as we think it should be answered, or does it rest rather on the character of a sovereign Lord? We can't really tell, can we, until we're in real trouble.

I never heard more from the young woman. I neglected to ask her address. But I prayed for her, asking God to enable her to show the world what genuine faith is—the kind of faith that overcomes the world because it trusts and obeys, no matter what the circumstances. The world does not want to be *told*. The world must be *shown*. Isn't that part of the answer to the great question of why Christians suffer?

Section Four

~~~

Our Culture
in Controversy

Two Views

One morning I received an article from a Christian magazine, written by a consulting physician at a well-known Christian clinic, entitled "Learning to Love Yourself." Ironically, in the same mail came a news magazine with its cover story, "The Curse of Self-Esteem."

I said, "Well." (That's a byword from my sister-in-law's family. When they think it best not to say what they're really thinking, but need to say *something,* they've found this useful: *I said, "Well."*)

The doctor's suggestions for improving your self-esteem included these: Praise yourself. Speak up for yourself. Believe in yourself. Be proud of yourself. Express total, unconditional acceptance for where you are at this moment.

The news magazine said, "If you're like most Americans, chances are you are at risk for low self-esteem. Sure, you felt bad at your kids' school's Career Day when you were the only parent who didn't own his own company. But unless your family psychometrician had ministered a Coopersmith Self-Esteem Inventory or the Kaplan Self-Derogation Scale you probably never imagined that a negative self-image might be holding you back in life. You just thought you were no good.

"But now you know that there are no bad people, only people who think badly of themselves."

"Aha," said I.

Then followed a few pithy quotes. Mark Twain: "Deep down in his heart no man much respects himself." Leo Tolstoy: "I am always with myself and it is I who am my tormentor." Goethe: "I do not know myself and God forbid that I should." And H.L. Mencken: "Self-respect—the secure feeling that no one, as yet, is suspicious."

To all of which I said, "Hear, hear."

As I paused and pondered I thought of the boy king Uzziah who, taking the throne at sixteen, made such a good start at obeying God and was "greatly helped until he became powerful.... His pride led to his downfall. He was unfaithful to the Lord his God," (2 Chronicles 26:15-16, NIV) and died a leper, excluded from the temple of the Lord. It was at the time of that ignominious death that the prophet Isaiah received his commission from God, for which he was prepared first by a vision of the Lord Himself, high and exalted. The very doorposts shook at the sound of the voices of the seraphim, *"Holy, holy, holy,"* and the prophet, in that awful revelation of the holiness of God, was given an instant and terrible self-revelation which wrenched from him the cry, "Woe is me!... I am ruined! For I am a man of unclean lips... and my eyes have seen the King, the Lord Almighty" (Isaiah 6:5, NIV).

That self of which the conscious image (of an *honest* man) is not merely "low" or "poor" but twisted, maimed, tortured, ruined— can it find wholeness and healing merely by sweet affirmation? It took fire from God's altar to cleanse Isaiah's lips. It took the total immolation of the Lamb to take away the sin of the world. Is the cross now obsolete?

"Beware of false prophets," Jesus warned (Matthew 7:15). "If anyone wants to follow in my footsteps he must give up all right to himself, take up his cross and follow me" (Matthew 16:24, Phillips). Can we manage to juggle the building of a stronger self-image while we fulfill those three conditions of discipleship?

"Whoever cares for his own safety is lost; but if a man will let himself be lost for My sake, he will find his true self" (Matthew 16:25, NEB). Who can forget about his own safety and allow himself to be lost while at one and the same time striving to build a stronger self-image? Sounds like a serious conflict of interest, doesn't it?

I know of nothing more agitating to the soul, nothing that so unsettles and disquiets, as the contemplation of the self. If I succeed in improving my self-image by minimizing my faults, I may find the peace that the world can give, but I will end up in spiritual turmoil. The peace of the penitent spirit is "very low in its own eyes, and therefore not unsettled" (Janet Erskine Stuart).

Those who follow the Lamb leave self behind, and "put on the new self, created to be like God in true righteousness and holiness" (Ephesians 4:24, NIV).

∞∞∞

I'm Dysfunctional,
You're Dysfunctional

P.T. Barnum knew what he was talking about when he said there's a sucker born every minute. He made money on it and so have thousands before and since. It isn't difficult to convince insecure people (who isn't insecure?) that they've been shabbily treated and deserved better. In fact they've been *horribly* treated and mistreated, misunderstood, misused, abused. Their families were *dysfunctional* (whose wasn't? whose parents did a perfect job?). No wonder they can't feel good about themselves. But here, folks, I can make you see that you're wonderful, really WONDER-FUL. It's bad to feel bad about yourself, and it's the fault of all those awful people who wounded you. You can just walk away from them.

As always, we must hold up whatever the world is saying to the straightedge of Scripture in order to see if it's crooked. The "gospel" according to the self-gurus, by which many will testify to having been helped, is very simple and, I believe, very crooked. The pathway to fulfillment is straight and narrow, and it begins at the cross where (as in *Pilgrim's Progress*) Christian drops his burden: the burden of sin, deep-rooted, infectious, malignant, death-dealing sin, the terrible root of all those "bad feelings." "Then was Christian glad and lightsome, and said, with a merry heart, 'He hath given me rest by His sorrow and life by His death.' Then he stood still a while to look and wonder; for it was very surprising to him, that the sight of the Cross should thus ease him of his burden."

Surprising it will always be to those who come to that Cross, and foolishness it will always be to those who don't. Rest comes by His sorrow, life by His death? Yes. "His purpose in dying for all was that men, while still in life, should cease to live for themselves and should live for him who for their sakes died and was raised to life. With us therefore worldly standards have ceased to count in our estimate of any man.... When anyone is united to Christ, there is a new world (or *a new act of creation*); the old order has gone, and a new order has already begun" (2 Corinthians 5:15-17, NEB).

That new order is a far cry from the notion of self-acceptance which has taken hold of the minds of many Christians. *Any message which makes the Cross redundant is anti-Christian.* The original sin, pride, is behind my "poor self-image," for I felt that I deserved better than I got, which is exactly what Eve felt! So it was pride, not poor self-image, that had to go. If I'm so beautiful and lovable, what was Jesus doing up there, nailed to the cross and crowned with thorns? Why all that hideous suffering for the pure Son of God? Here's why: There was *no other way* to deliver us from the hell of our own proud self-loving selves, no other way out of the bondage of self-pity and self-congratulation. How shall we take our stand beneath the cross of Jesus and continue to love the selves that put Him there? How can we survey the wondrous cross and at the same time feed our pride? No. It won't work. Jesus put it simply: If you want to be My disciple, you must leave self behind, take up the cross, and follow Me.

George MacDonald writes, "Right gladly would He free them from their misery, but He knows only one way: He will teach them to be like himself, meek and lowly, bearing with gladness the yoke of His Father's will. This is the one, the only right, the only possible way of freeing them from their sin, the cause of their unrest."

∞∞∞

The Taking of
Human Life

In the relentless effort to keep the world from squeezing me into its own mold (see Romans 12:1-2, Phillips) my mind is always making comparisons and connections and trying to test the world's reasoning by the straightedge of Scripture. When I read of the execution in Texas of Charles Brooks, Jr., by lethal injection, I made one of those connections. I remembered another news story a few months before about an unborn twin who was quietly dispatched, by means of a needle in its heart, while still in its mother's womb. Medical science has advanced to the stage where it is possible to remove human beings from this world's scene cleanly and kindly (we tell ourselves) and without too much trauma to the executioners and the consenting public. Of the trauma to the victim we prefer not to let ourselves think too much.

One of the people I refer to, of course, was a full-grown man, convicted of murder. The other was far from full-grown. It was not even born. Nobody wanted it to be born because it happened to be not quite normal. A person, without question, but not quite a normal person. So, since the mother very much wanted the normal twin to be born, she was very glad to be able to get rid of the abnormal one in such a handy way.

In a *Time* (Dec. 20, 1982) essay about the Brooks execution, Roger Rosenblatt writes of the public's eagerness for a "gentle killing," yet its hunger also to know the details of the prisoner's last dinner and last words, his position on the stretcher, and how the tubes were hooked up which would carry the poison into his bloodstream. Strange that there should be this fascination at a time when there is strong protest, at least in the media, against the death penalty for criminals. There is no protest in major magazines against the death penalty for unborn children and no corresponding eagerness for pictures or descriptions of just how it is done. Few people are willing to scrutinize the details of what happens to the tiny bodies who are daily, at the request of their mothers, and with the consent of the Supreme Court, being disposed of by sophisticated chemical, pharmaceutical, and mechanical techniques.

The correction facility in Texas and the abortion facilities in hospitals are equally thorough in their efforts to make sure that the method *works*. Imagine the embarrassment if Charles Brooks had managed to slip out of the straps that bound him to the gurney, or if the silent fluid had somehow been obstructed in the tubes! Nobody wants that to happen. It is a major disaster, too, when an abortion produces a living child instead of a dead one. Some awful scenes have taken place in hospital nurseries when a baby has been taken there who had been intended for the garbage can. What is wanted in the cases of both the murderer and the undesirable fetus is death, pure death, the "spectacle of life removed."

Do not misunderstand me. I believe that capital punishment is both necessary and just. I believe that abortion is murder. Both are appalling to anyone human, it seems to me. Surely, no matter what our convictions and public declarations may be, we shrink inside at the hideousness of it all. But one is commanded by God—evil must be dealt with by public justice—and the other is forbidden. We cannot, without His express direction, take human life into our hands. Let us not imagine that we can somehow palliate the stark and shocking fact of death by making it private. Only a few people, including four reporters and Brook's girlfriend, were allowed to witness his death. An abortion is now called a *private matter*, to be decided solely by a woman and her physician. Let us not, by making it quick, easy, and clean, evade the truth that somebody is being killed.

Rosenblatt in his essay looks for the day when we may "drive out the barbarians." Is it barbaric, then, to mete out judgment in this form to a murderer, but somehow civilized to send a lethal poison into the heart of an as yet sinless child?

Paul wrote to the young minister Timothy to warn him of the sort of evil he must guard against. "Men will love nothing but money and self... men who put pleasure in the place of God, men who preserve the outward form of religion but are a standing denial of its reality. Keep clear of men like these.... These men defy the truth, they have lost the power to reason, and they cannot pass the tests of faith" (2 Timothy 3:2, 5-6, 8-9, NEB). God help us not only to stand for the truth, but to obey it scrupulously that we may not lose the power to think as Christians.

∽∽∽

Give Them Parking Space But Let Them Starve to Death

Another moral threshold was crossed when a tiny baby boy, at the specific request of his parents and with the sanction of the Supreme Court of Indiana, was starved to death in a hospital. "Infant Doe" (he was not allowed the usual recognition of being human by being named), born with Down's syndrome and a malfunctioning esophagus (the latter could have been corrected with surgery), died, as the *Washington Post* (April 18) stated, "not because he couldn't sustain life without a million dollars worth of medical machinery, but because no one fed him." For six days the nurses in that Bloomington hospital went about their usual routines of bathing and changing and feeding all the newborns except one. They bathed and changed Baby Doe but they never gave him a bottle. Over his crib was a notice, DO NOT FEED. Several couples came forward, begging to be allowed to adopt him. They were turned down.

What went on in that little box during those six terrible days and nights? We turn our imagination away. It's unthinkable. But if I were to think about it, and put down on paper what my mind saw, I would be accused of playing on people's feelings, and of making infanticide (yes, *infanticide*—call it what it is) an "emotional issue." Let me suppose at least that the baby cried—quite loudly (at first). One report says that he was placed in a room alone, lest his crying disturb others (others, perhaps, who were capable of helping him).

Joseph Sobran, in his column in the Los Angeles Times Syndicate, suggested that "opposition to infanticide will soon be deplored as the dogma of a few religious sects who want to impose their views on everyone else." The language sounds sickeningly familiar.

There has been a conspicuous silence from those who usually raise shrill protest when other human rights are violated—the rights of smokers, homosexuals, and criminals are often as loudly insisted upon as those of children, women, and the handicapped.

The handicapped? What on earth is happening when a society is so careful to provide premium parking spaces to make things easier for them, but sees no smallest inconsistency when one of them who happens to be too young to scream, "For God's sake, feed me!" is quietly murdered? It is in the name of humanity, humaneness, compassion, and freedom that these things occur, but never is it acknowledged that the real reasons are comfort and convenience, that is, simple selfishness. "Abortion not only prefers comfort, convenience, or advantage of the pregnant woman to the very life of her unborn child, a fundamentally good thing, but seeks to deny that the life ever existed. In this sense it is a radical denial not only of the worth of a specific life but of the essential goodness of life itself and the Providential ordering of its procreation" (R.V. Young, "Taking Choice Seriously," *The Human Life Review*, Vol. VIII, no. 3.)

But weren't we talking about infanticide and haven't we now switched to abortion? The premises on which abortion is justified are fundamentally the same on which infanticide is seen as civilized and acceptable. What Hitler used to call eugenics is now called "quality of life," never mind whether the life in question happens to be the mother's or the child's. Death, according to three doctors who put the issue out into the open in the *New England Journal of Medicine* in 1973, is now considered an option in the "treatment" of infants; in other words, a mortuary may now replace the nursery. One cannot help thinking of the antiseptic "shower rooms" of the Third Reich, where the unwanted were "treated" to death. Nor can one forget the words of Jesus,

"Inasmuch as ye have done it unto one of the least of these my brethren, ye have done it unto me" (Matthew 25:40, KJV).

Can any Christian argue that the smallest and most defenseless are, by virtue merely of being too small and too defenseless, not His brethren?

∞∞∞

What Is Happening?

What on earth is happening in our culture? The answer is plain, I'm afraid, in Romans 1 and 2. Men render truth dumb and inoperative by their wickedness. They refuse to acknowledge God or to thank Him for what He is or does. They become fatuous in their argumentations. Behind a facade of wisdom they become fools. They give up God. They forfeit the truth of God and accept a lie. They overflow with insolent pride; their minds teem with diabolical invention. They recognize no obligations to honor, lose all natural affection, and have no use for mercy. They do not hesitate to give their thorough approval to others who do the same (see Romans 1:18-2:5, Phillips).

Can we condemn them without subjecting ourselves to the same standard of judgment by which we condemn? Of course we can't. Judgment must be *righteous judgment* (John 7:24), based on the Word of God.

"There is no doubt at all that he will 'render to every man according to his works,'" and that means eternal life to those who, in patiently doing good, aim at the unseen.... "It also means anger and wrath for those who rebel against God's plan of life. "But there is glory and honor and peace for every worker on the side of good" (see Rom 2:6-10, Phillips).

Stilled now be every anxious care;
See God's great goodness everywhere;
Leave all to Him in perfect rest:
He will do all things for the best.
From the German

CRRD

Can Birth Be Wrong?

The wildest science fiction cannot exceed in outrage some of the legal precedents that have been set in the past few decades. I read in a magazine about "wrongful birth" suits, in which parents sue a physician because their child was born as a result of practitioner negligence: for example, a failed vasectomy, failed abortion (a "failed" abortion, don't forget, means one in which the child destined for the scrap heap happens to be born alive and kicking, so to speak), or failure by the physician to provide parents with adequate contraceptive methods.

There are also "wrongful life" suits in which the *child* sues the physician because he would have been better off not to be born at all. His very life is "wrongful." The child, in other words, had a right not to be born. How, exactly, would the court measure damages in the case of a healthy child? There would have been awards if there were defects.

The only good news in this appalling article was that in a wrongful birth case in Illinois in 1979 the court held that the birth of a healthy child is an esteemed right and not a compensable wrong. In England, at least up until the spring of 1983, the decision had been that entry into life should not be the basis for legal action.

"O Lord my heart is not proud, nor are my eyes haughty," wrote the psalmist (131:1, NEB), "I do not busy myself with great matters or things to marvelous for me." I am afraid we tamper far too much with the mysteries of life and death, instead of leaving them to Him who holds the keys.

∽∞∽

An Unaborted Gift

An African Christian wrote a friend in the U.S.: "We have six children. We had agreed to stop having other children. We even started family planning after the last was born, but (and a big 'but') we found out that C. was pregnant. I don't know what really happened. My wife and I started crying because we did not know what to do. We have been asking God and telling Him that six children were enough for us. However we were later comforted by God Himself because He said that He will never leave us and will protect us with the young ones. I therefore ask you to pray for us. C. is expecting the child in about three months. Remember we were not ready for this baby. Pray that we will be able to joyfully receive the baby as a gift from the almighty God. It is my prayer that my wife will be able to bear all that burden and that the baby will be a blessing to us. You know we have two boys with sickle cells. Please pray with us that God will not give us another such child. Brethren, I have been suffering with these sick boys and we don't like another one of that type. It will just finish us. We have many sleepless nights every year because of these sons when they are in pains.... With all that I am happy to tell you that there is nothing which will separate me from the Love of God.... Pray, pray for us. God bless you all."

I don't know this man, but I have prayed for him, and for all others who, with what the world would call "good reasons for abortion," receive the child from Him who made it, and who said, "Whoever receives one of these children in My name, receives Me" (Mark 9:36, NEB).

∞∞∞

Disposable Children

A ruling of the Internal Revenue Service now allows parents a tax exemption if a child intended for abortion lives for any length of time. The breathtakingly fancy mental footwork necessary to justify such action goes something like this: what was meant to be discarded is not a child. It is called a "p.o.c." (product of conception, which of course is what children and all the rest of us are). The bad news is that this disposable tissue turned out to be a child and (alas) was *born.* The good news is that you can get a tax exemption for a dependent child. The best news is that its dependence is only temporary. Call it a child, then, till you get your money. You need not go to the trouble of keeping it. You can call it tissue again and toss it out. Thus the abortionist's mistake becomes the taxpayer's windfall, and the doctor who orders the child abandoned (i.e., killed by neglect and sometimes by active means) is not charged with murder but paid for what is now called a postnatal abortion. Will you stand up against the outrage called "pro-choice"? Do you understand its implications?

"Because they have not seen fit to acknowledge God, he has given them up to their own depraved reason. This leads them to break all the rules of conduct. They are filled with every kind of injustice, mischief, rapacity, and malice.... They are without natural affection and without pity" (Romans 1:28, 29, 31, NEB).

∽∽∽∽

A New Medical Breakthrough

As I mentioned earlier, some time ago I read of a new medical triumph involving unborn twins. Amniocentesis had shown that one of them had Down's syndrome. The mother decided she did not want that child, so with the simple expedient of piercing the heart of the baby with a long needle, it was killed in the womb. She carried the twins to term and delivered one child alive—the one she wanted to keep—and one child dead—the one she didn't want to keep. This was hailed as a remarkable breakthrough. I would ask you to pause for a moment here and consider this question: what was it, exactly, that was killed? What was it that was not killed? The answer to both questions, of course, is—a child. They were both children. They were twins. I used plain, ordinary words to tell the story—the words the news report used. Nothing ambiguous. Nothing incendiary.

I read the following week in the same magazine about another medical breakthrough. This time doctors had used an instrument inserted into a womb not to kill a child but to save one. This child had a serious heart anomaly which they were able to correct with intrauterine surgery. Can any honest and reasonable person fail to make the comparison here? In the second case, the instrument in the surgeon's hand enabled the tiny heart to keep on working. In the first case, the needle in the surgeon's hand made the heart quit working. What, exactly, should we call that?

The intrauterine surgery was called *lifesaving* because they fixed a baby's defective heart. What language are we allowed to use when we speak of destroying a heart that's working perfectly! There is a simple and obvious word, but we are not allowed to use it. Well, what about *life-destroying?* Is that permissible for this neat and efficient technique? Well, not really. Because the word *life* is explosive. Life is not relevant here. It's the mother's life that we are supposed to consider, nobody else's. The other isn't a life—not one worth living anyway, not one worth the mother's suffering for. So we must not use the ordinary words. They're too emotional. They're loaded. The fact is they stopped the heart. That's all. Just made it quit beating.

I was glad that the writer of the article on the baby whose heart was corrected acknowledged the possibility that fetal surgery might raise an ethical question which the medical world thought it had laid to rest. Might it be necessary, in view of these advances, to ask all over again whether a fetus is a person?

This is the issue today. It is, in the final analysis, the only question that needs to be considered when we speak of the unborn. Is the thing disposable? Is it an object with no life of its own, a bit of tissue which belongs to a woman who has the right to do with it what she chooses? If she needs it and wants it, she keeps it. If she doesn't need it and doesn't want it, she throws it out. So what's all the shouting about?

Truthfulness is the willingness to accept facts. Truthtellers are always regarded as either ridiculous, or so dangerous as to deserve death. "No truth," wrote Hannah Arendt, "that crosses someone's profit, ambition, or lust, is permissible. Unwelcome facts possess an infuriating stubbornness that nothing can move except plain lies."

Here are the unwelcome facts. We were talking about children: the twin who was saved, the child with the defective heart who was also saved, and the twin whose heart was pierced with a needle. They were children. Choices were made regarding those children: deliberate, conscious choices. One, to allow a child to live. Another, to intervene surgically so that a child might live who would otherwise die. (Would the surgeon who performed that operation have dreamed of telling the mother that her baby was not a person? He saved its life, and the mother was grateful.) But in the other case, what was the choice? It was to kill a child. These are the unwelcome facts, but they are infuriatingly stubborn. They will not go away. It was a child. It was killed. Nothing will move those facts except lies.

I ask you earnestly to look at the little creature with eyes and hands and beating heart, held in that safest of places, the mother's womb. No woman who holds such a thing within her doubts that she holds a child. No doctor who extracts it by whatever swift and putatively safe means can deny that what he extracts is a human being, and that what he does is to kill it.

I ask you for God's sake to look at the truth. And I ask you, finally, to think about what Jesus said: "I tell you solemnly, in so far as you did this to one of the least of these brothers of mine, you did it to me" (Matthew 25:40, JB). Jesus will not forget.

CXXXD

Women: The Road Ahead

A special issue of a leading news magazine had this title for its theme. There were pictures of women in prison with babies; an inconsolable "crack" baby with a tangle of tubes connected to machines, crying his little heart out; a mother charged with a felony: delivery of drugs to her newborn child; women in politics "sharing real rather than cosmetic power;" a veiled Muslim woman; ten tough-minded women who "create individual rules for success," *e.g.* a police chief, a bishop, a rock climber, a baseball club owner, a rap artist, a fashion tycoon, an Indian chief, and others. There were single mothers, lesbian mothers, divorced mothers, working (outside the home) mothers. There was a twelve-year-old who fixes supper for her sisters when Mom works late, and there was a man who is a househusband. But there was not one picture of a father and mother and their children. Not one.

"A jockstrap was a parting gift when Marion Howington retired last year from the once all-male post of senior v.p. at J. Walter Thompson.... For Howington, a striking 60, who began climbing the agency's ladder in Chicago in 1967, the key to success was to 'be aggressive' and 'think like a man.'...

'There's not a woman anywhere who made it in business who is not tough, self-centered, and enormously aggressive.'"

Readers occasionally ask me why I write about horrifying stuff. Well, to precipitate prayer and to remind us that we do not engage in a war against mere flesh and blood. As Ephesians 6 says, "We are up against the unseen power that controls this dark world, and spiritual agents from the headquarters of evil.... Take your stand then with truth as your belt, righteousness your breastplate, the Gospel of peace firmly on your feet, salvation as your helmet and in your hand the sword of the Spirit, the Word of God" (PHILLIPS).

There was at least one bright note in that special issue. Sixty-six percent of women aged 18-24 answered yes to the question, "If you had the opportunity, would you be interested in staying at home and raising children?" They are beginning to see that the corporate world is no day at the beach. There was encouragement also in a letter to Ann Landers from a former executive: "It suddenly dawned on me that I had my priorities bollixed up and my children deserve better. I had to admit getting fulfillment from my career was a pipe dream. It may elude me in motherhood as well, but I now know what really matters. After nine years of paying someone to raise my children, I was forced to admit my family is more important to me than anything else. I wish I had known this when my first child was born. I am now thirty-six years old and happy to say we are expecting our third child.... This means cutting down on vacations, and our entertaining will be reduced to popcorn and video parties with a few old friends.... 'No success in life can compensate for failure at home.'"

I had a letter from one who made it her goal to be like the godly woman of Titus 2:3-5. As usual, when one determines to obey the Lord "the enemy was there causing me to feel like my whole world is on a roller-coaster, that my family was not important, that I am worthless, lazy, because I am a homemaker. I was so tired sometimes I could barely get meals on the table. I heard remarks like, 'Oh, you aren't working at all? How do you manage to live on one income? It's hard on your husband! What do you do all day? You must be bored!'

"As my husband and I listened to your program we reaffirmed the goals we had set and committed them to the Lord once more.... Pray for me to be strong and of good courage and to remain faithful, with an attitude of submission, a true handmaid of the Lord."

Women need to be prayed for. They need all the encouragement they can get. Sadly, it is not always forthcoming even from other Christians. I saw a lovely girl in the market the other day with the sweetest of sweet baby girls in her grocery cart. I asked about the baby—five months old, her only child so far. "Are you able to stay home to care for her?" "Oh yes! Oh, I can't even imagine putting her in day care." I gave her my blessing. Perhaps even a brief word from a stranger can make a difference to a young mother.

Prayer lays hold of God's plan and becomes the link between His will and its accomplishment on earth. Things happen which would not happen without prayer. Let's not forget that. Amazing things happen, and we are given the privilege of being the channels of the Holy Spirit's prayer. As we pray *against* abortion and pornography and homosexuality and divorce and drugs and *for* the strengthening of homes and families, we often feel helpless and hopeless until we remember, "We do not know how to pray worthily as sons of God, but his Spirit within us is actually praying for us in those agonizing longings which never find words" (Romans 8:26, PHILLIPS).

Section Five

The Christian
Home

In my attempts to promote the comfort of my family, the quiet of my spirit has been disturbed. Some of this is doubtless owing to physical weakness; but, with every temptation, there is a way of escape; there is never any need to sin. Another thing I have suffered loss from—entering into the business of the day without seeking to have my spirit quieted and directed. So many things press upon me, this is sometimes neglected; shame to me that it should be so.

This is of great importance, to watch carefully—now I am so weak—not to over fatigue myself, because then I cannot contribute to the pleasure of others; and a placid face and a gentle tone will make my family more happy than anything else I can do for them. Our own will gets sadly into the performance of our duties sometimes.

Elizabeth T. King

Contexts

A writer in the *New Yorker* some time ago analyzed television as "the context of no-context." Think about that one. The only context in which the words are coming at us from the tube is our living room or kitchen, which has nothing whatever to do with the speaker. The speaker's backdrop is usually a TV studio, which we know is a mock-up. So we are excused from evaluating what is said in terms of context. There is none.

In what context does a Christian live, move, act, think, decide? It must be the context of God's Kingdom. We either live in that Kingdom, or we live in the world; we either take our cues from the Bible or from the media; we set our goals according to what is going to matter forever or according to the quotation of the day.

Think, in the context of the kingdom of God, about this actual incident in a public school classroom: The teacher asked each child what his mother did. There was only one child whose mother did not work outside the home.

Teacher: Oh, so what does your mother do?

Child: She—um, well, you know, she does, um, stuff around the house.

Teacher: You mean she cooks and cleans? She irons clothes, makes beds?

Child: Yes.

Teacher: So you could say, then, that you have a *traditional* mother, is that right?

Child: Yes.

Teacher:(with a long, searching look) And do you *like* that?

Consider the context from which that teacher's questions come. It is not one which recognizes any divine design for the home, any glory in service, any joyful willingness to do humble work without thought of gain or appreciation. Consider the pressure put on a little child to question the only context his life has had, the context which has until now meant security, normalcy, and happiness for him. He will be wondering if his mother is some sort of an oddity, his home not an ordinary one.

It is not for nothing that the classic passage on the warfare of the Christian immediately follows Paul's specific instructions about intimate human relationships: wives, submit; husbands, love; fathers, do not goad your children to resentment. These are the areas of most vicious and relentless attack. The Christian home is a stronghold, and the enemy will never let up his attempts to undermine it or breach its sanctity.

"Put on all the armor which God provides, so that you may be able to stand firm against the devices of the devil. For our fight is not against human foes [corrupt government officials, public school boards, for example, or even an impossible-to-live-with spouse or teenager] but against cosmic powers, against the authorities and potentates of this dark world, against the superhuman forces of evil in the heavens. Therefore take God's armor..." (Ephesians 6:11-13, NEB).

Prayer is a powerful weapon. It is an indispensable weapon. It takes practice to wield it. It takes courage and time and spiritual energy.

⎯⎯⎯

My Mother

She was Kath to her close friends, Dearie to my father, and always Mother (never Mom) to her six children. She held us on her lap when we were small and rocked us, sang to us, and told us stories. We begged for the ones about "when you were a little girl." Katharine Gillingham was born June 21, 1899 in Philadelphia. We loved hearing about the butler who did tricks for her behind her parents' backs and about the alarmed postman who rushed to rescue the screaming child with her arm down a dog's throat until he heard what the child was saying: "He's got my *peanut!*" In 1922 she married Philip E. Howard Jr., a man who, because he had lost an eye in an accident, felt sure no woman would have him. They worked for five years with the Belgian Gospel Mission, then returned to the States when he became associate editor (later editor) of *The Sunday School Times.*

Mother's course was finished on February 7, 1987. She was up and dressed as usual in the morning at the Quarryville Presbyterian Home in Pennsylvania, made it to lunch with the help of her walker, lay down afterwards, having remarked rather matter-of-factly to someone that she knew she was dying, and wondered where her husband was. Later in the afternoon cardiac arrest took her, very quietly.

Each of us (in chronological order) took a few minutes at the funeral to speak of some aspect of Mother's character. Phil spoke of her consistency and unfailing availability as a mother; of her love for Dad ("He was always my lover," she said). I recalled how she used to mop her eyes at the table, laughing till she cried at some of my father's bizarre descriptions, or even at his oft-told jokes; how she was obedient to the New Testament pattern of godly womanhood, including hospitality. Dave talked about her unreserved surrender to the Lord, first of herself (at Stony Brook conference in New York, and then, painfully, years later at Prairie Bible Institute in Canada) of her children; of how, when we left home, she followed us not only with prayer but, for forty years with hardly a break, with a weekly letter. Ginny told how Mother's example taught her what it means to be a lady; how to discipline herself, her children, her home. Tom remembered the books she read to us (A.A. Milne, Beatrix Potter, *Sir Knight of the Splendid Way*, for example), and the songs she sang as she rocked each of us little children ("Safe in the Arms of Jesus," "Go Tell Aunt Nancy"), shaping our vision of life. Jim pictured her sitting in her small cane rocker in the bay window of her bedroom after the breakfast dishes were done, sitting quietly before the Lord with the Bible, *Daily Light*, and notebook.

The last three years were sorrowful ones for all of us. Arteriosclerosis had done its work in her mind and she was confused and lonely ("Why hasn't Dad been to see me?" "He's been with the Lord for 23 years, Mother." "Nobody told me!") Still a lady, she tried to be neatly groomed, always offered a chair to those who came. She had not lost her humor, her almost unbeatable skill at Scrabble, her ability to play the piano, sing hymns, and remember her children. But she wanted us to pray that the Lord would let her go Home, so we did.

The funeral ended with the six of us singing "The Strife is O'er," then all family members, including our beloved aunts Alice and Anne Howard, sang "To God Be the Glory." The graveside service closed with the Doxology (the one with Alleluias). We think of her now, loving us with an even greater love, her poor frail mortality left behind, her eyes beholding the King in His beauty. "If you knew what God knows about death," wrote George MacDonald, "you would clap your listless hands."

∽∽

Family Prayers

When I was a child my father and mother gathered the six of us in the living room after breakfast every morning for family prayers. First we sang a hymn, omitting none of the stanzas, accompanied on the piano by one of our parents. It was in this way that we learned a good bit of solid theology without any conscious effort. I must emphasize that it was *hymns* and old gospel songs we sang at home. There was not much place then for choruses or gospel ditties.

There are some young families who still do this today. Judy Palpant of Spokane, who had heard me tell about our family prayers, writes, "Our children know that you were the inspiration for our three-year-old tradition of singing a hymn with our family devotions. We sing the same one each morning for a month. Tonight was the first time we tabulated the number of hymns we had learned. The children were impressed! Let me assure you that many new words and truths have been impressed upon their hearts and minds as we have discussed the themes and words of our chosen hymn. Our many guests at breakfast (especially when we were in Africa) were often blessed by the singing of a hymn. My husband's parents were visiting us when we were singing 'Savior, Like a Shepherd Lead Us.' That hymn was sung at their wedding. During the Easter season one year we were learning 'When I Survey the Wondrous Cross on Which the Prince of Glory Died.' A missionary from Kenya underlined the words 'Prince of Glory' for us by sharing some insights with us. Thank you for this idea which has enriched our family as well as our guests."

A reader asks, "At what age were the children when your parents started family prayers? How long a passage was read?" I think they must have begun as soon as the first child was born. I am Number Two, and I can't remember a time when we did not have family prayers. All of us were included, the smaller ones sitting on laps. My father read from Hurlbut's *Story of the Bible* (wearing out three hardback copies!), just a page or so each morning. In the evening after dinner he read the evening portion of *Daily Light*, which is pure Scripture (King James Version). The hymn came first, then reading, then (in the mornings, because we were not around the table then) we knelt to pray, my father leading, all joining in the Lord's Prayer to close.

This question from another reader: "How can I encourage my husband as the spiritual leader of the family to have regular family devotions?" This is one I am often asked. If he is a Christian I would hope that he is willing at least to listen to his wife's suggestion. Many men believe their wives are "more spiritual" than they, and feel justified in leaving spiritual training of the children up to them. This is a mistake. The father is the priest in the home. He is the head of his wife. It is his God-given assignment to take spiritual leadership. No matter how brief and simple the devotional time may be, there is no calculating the power of its long-term effect on the children. They learn very early the place God has in their parents' lives.

My father was a very simple man—humble, honest about his faith, but reticent in the extreme about speaking of it. We had no such thing as "sharing times" in our family. It was rare for us to converse about spiritual things, especially personal experience. But we knew our parents prayed in private, read their Bibles, and prayed and read aloud with us. It was routine. But it mattered. It matters to me now. I hope perhaps these words of testimony may nudge some of those reticent Christian fathers to take courage, take the bull by the horns, and say, "I've learned something. It's important. More important, maybe, than anything else we do in this house. We're going to start today."

CRGRO

Drudgery

"I must admit I feel a lot of pressure with two children under two years of age. I am committed to do it until they are in school, however, and feel it is God's will. At times like this—when I wonder if I will even be able to finish this letter with both of them screaming for something—or when I miss going to lunch or getting dressed up, everyday life seems a drudgery. I worked hard to get through college—to be a scrubwoman, ha!"

I understand this mother's cry. So does the Lord. He has given us this word: "No temptation has come your way that is too hard for flesh and blood to bear. But God can be trusted not to allow you to suffer any temptation beyond your powers of endurance. He will see to it that every temptation has a way out, so that it will never be impossible for you to bear it" (1 Corinthians 10:13, PHILLIPS).

"A *way out!*" I can hear her say, "What mother has a way out?"

The New English Bible translation throws light on this: "a way out, *by enabling you to sustain it.*" Think, too, of Jesus' words, "My yoke is casy and my burden is light" (Matthew 11:29 AV). He is willing to bear our burdens with us, if only we will come to Him and share the yoke, His yoke.

I saw this principle in operation when I visited the Dohnavur Fellowship in India. There, day after day, year in and year out, Indian women (most of them single) care for little children, handicapped children, infirm adults, old folks. They don't go anywhere. They have none of our usual forms of amusement and diversion. They work with extremely primitive equipment—there is no running water, for example, no stoves but wood-burning ones, no washing machines. In one of the buildings I saw this text: "There they dwelt with the King for His work." That's the secret. They do it for Him. They ask for and receive His grace to do it. I saw the joy in their lovely faces.

Sunday Morning

Sunday mornings can be a real test of a mother's sanctification, especially if her husband happens to be a pastor who leaves the house much earlier than the rest of the family. Here's how it went recently in one house (you're free to speculate on whose):

The fifteen-year-old couldn't tuck his shirt in because of "something to do with the pockets," and his belt was too small.

The thirteen-year-old was having trouble curling her hair.

The ten-year-old couldn't find her Sunday School lesson.

The eight-year-old hadn't done his Bible readings because he didn't know which they were.

The six-year-old's room and closet were unacceptably messy, and the socks she had on were muddy.

The three-year-old couldn't find her Bible. Although not yet a reader, she couldn't think of going to church without the Bible.

The baby's carrying blanket had disappeared.

Somehow the mother was to be nicely groomed, calm, and able to get this whole package into a van, seated and belted as law requires, and drive them to church on time.

But everything in this scene is the King's Business, which He looks on in loving sympathy and understanding, for, as Baron Von Hugel said, "The chain of cause and effect which makes up human life, is bisected at every point by a vertical line relating us and all we do to God." *This* is what He has given us to do, this task here on this earth, not the task we aspired to do, but this one. The absurdities involved cut us down to size. The great discrepancy between what we envisioned and what we've got force us to be *real*. And

God is our great Reality, more real than the realest of earthly conditions, an unchanging Reality. It is His providence that has put us where we are. It's where we belong. It is for us to receive it—all of it—humbly, quietly, thankfully.

Sunday morning, the Lord's Day, can be the very time when everything seems so utterly unrelated to the world of the spirit that it is simply ridiculous. Yet to the Lord's lovers it is only a *seeming*. Everything is an affair of the spirit. Everything, to one who loves God and longs with a sometimes desperate longing for a draught of Living Water, a single touch of His hand, a quiet word—everything, I say, can be seen in His perspective.

Does He watch? Yes, "Thou God seest me" (Genesis 16:3, KJV). Is His love surrounding us? "I have loved thee with an everlasting love" (Jeremiah 31:3, KJV). "I will never leave thee or forsake thee" (Hebrews 13:5, KJV). May I offer to Him my feeling of the dislocation between reality and my ideals, that great chasm which separates the person I long to be, the work I long to do for Him, the family I struggle to perfect for His glory—from the actuality? I may indeed, for it is God Himself who stirs my heart to desire, and *He* can easily see across the chasm. He enfolds all of it, He is at work in me and in those I pray for, "to will and to do of his good pleasure" (Philippians 2:13, KJV). I may take heart, send up an instant look of gratitude, and—well, get that beloved flock into the van and head down the freeway singing!

Sir Thomas Browne wrote, "Man is incurably amphibious; he belongs to two worlds—to two sets of duties, needs, and satisfactions—to the Visible or This World, and to the Invisible or Other World" (*Essays and Addresses*, 2nd series).

∞∞∞

A Word for Fathers

While visiting Columbia Bible College in South Carolina, I found in the library a little book called *Father and Son,* written by my grandfather, Philip E. Howard. He writes:

"Do you remember that encouraging word of Thomas Fuller's, a chaplain of Oliver Cromwell's time? It's a good passage for a father in all humility and gratitude to tuck away in his memory treasures:

"'Lord, I find the genealogy of my Savior strangely checkered with four remarkable changes in four immediate generations. (1) Rehoboam begat Abijah; that is, a bad father begat a bad son. (2) Abijah begat Asa; that is, a bad father begat a good son. (3) Asa begat Jehoshaphat; that is, a good father a good son. (4) Jehoshaphat begat Joram; that is, a good father a bad son. I see, Lord, from hence that my father's piety cannot be entailed; that is bad news for me. But I see also that actual impiety is not always hereditary; that is good news for my son.'"

In another chapter Grandpa Howard tells this story.

"A sensitive, timid little boy, long years ago, was accustomed to lie down to sleep in a low 'trundle-bed,' which was rolled under his parents' bed by day and was brought out for his use by night. As he lay there by himself in the darkness, he could hear the voices of his parents, in their lighted sitting-room across the hallway, on the other side of the house. It seemed to him that his parents never slept; for he left them awake when he was put to bed at night, and he found them awake when he left his bed in the morning. So far this thought was a cause of cheer to him, as his mind was busy with imaginings in the weird darkness of his lonely room.

"After loving good-night words and kisses had been given him by both his parents, and he had nestled down to rest, this little boy was accustomed, night after night, to rouse up once more, and to call out from his trundle-bed to his strong-armed father, in the room from which the light gleamed out, beyond the shadowy hallway, 'Are you there, papa?' And the answer would come back cheerily, 'Yes, my child, I am here.' 'You'll take care of me tonight, papa, won't you?' was then the question. 'Yes, I'll take care of you, my child,' was the comforting response. 'Go to sleep now. Good night.' And the little fellow would fall asleep restfully, in the thought of those assuring good-night words.

"A little matter that was to the loving father; but it was a great matter to the sensitive son. It helped to shape the son's life. It gave the father an added hold on him; and it opened up the way for his clearer understanding of his dependence on the loving watchfulness of the All-Father. And to this day when that son, himself a father and a grandfather, lies down to sleep at night, he is accustomed, out of the memories of that lesson of long ago, to look up through the shadows of his earthly sleeping place into the far-off light of his Father's presence, and to call out, in the same spirit of childlike trust and helplessness as so long ago, 'Father, you'll take care of me tonight, won't you?'" And he hears the assuring answer come back, 'He that keepeth thee will not slumber. The Lord shall keep thee from all evil. He shall keep thy soul. Sleep, my child, in peace.' And so he realizes the twofold blessing of a father's goodnight words."

That story, says Grandpa, came from his own father-in-law, my great-grandfather, Henry Clay Trumbull. I have a hunch that Trumbull was that little boy, and the father my great-great-grandfather.

CRCRD

What Is a Wife to Do?

M any women write to me about their husbands—some of them so thankful for the godly men they've been given, some of them deeply troubled by ungodly behavior. I hear stories of professing Christians, pastors, church leaders who abuse their wives, neglect their children, spend money foolishly, etc. Recently several have written about men who habitually indulge in sexual sin of one sort or another. Usually the wife tells me she has confronted him with God's word, requested that he desist, begged him to submit to Christian counseling, discussed the deleterious effect it has on their marriage, and asked him to understand how deeply he is hurting those who love him. He turns a deaf ear.

What is a *wife* to do? *That* is the question I am asked. If I were asked what the husbands should do the answer would be simple: quit it. When I say simple, of course, I do not mean easy. First a man must repent and admit his helplessness, which may be harder for a man than for a woman. Then he may be willing to accept the help of others who have walked the same path. Accountability and encouragement can help him see his sin for what it is.

God has given us a will, and promises the strength to say no to temptation. He never allows us to be tempted beyond our ability to resist. He will give us all the help we are *willing* to receive. "I will obey your decrees. I call out to you; save me and I will keep your statutes. I rise before dawn and cry for help; I have put my hope in your word. My eyes stay open through the watches of the night, that I may meditate on your promises" (Psalm 119:145-148, NIV). The man whose temptation is pornography, for example, is not *forced* to go to the blue movie, open the pornographic mail or magazine, or visit the "adult" bookstore. But he, of course, is not asking me or anyone else for advice. He doesn't want it. No amount of counseling, professional or otherwise, will change his lust unless he is willing to be changed. There must be a readiness to do what God says. "It is God's will that you should be sanctified: that you should avoid sexual immorality; that each of you should learn to control his own body in a way that is holy and honorable, not in passionate lust like the heathen" (1 Thessalonians 4:3-5, NIV). That is what God has to say about it, and He has never given a command which He will not enable us to obey. It is *always* possible to do the will of God.

In some cases the wife has not felt that it was *her* duty to confront him. While my first impulse was to say she should, further thought and prayer convinced me that she may be right. Are we not to have a gentle and quiet spirit? Is it the wife's place to confront, in view of 1 Peter 3:1-2; 6? "[Your husbands] may be won over without words by the behavior of their wives, when they see the purity and reverence of your lives.... You are [Sarah's] daughters if you do what is right and do not give way to fear" (NIV). Things that are impossible with us are possible with God. He is in the business of changing men's hearts and transforming lives—often in answer to a wife's prayers.

It may not be amiss for the wife to seek human help, perhaps in a spiritual "mother," a woman who has walked with God for years and knows how to pray and how to keep a confidence. If professional counseling is sought, let it be truly Christian, i.e. Christ-centered, cross-centered. This week I received a letter from a woman who had had an apparently immovable obstacle in her relationship with her husband. She had struggled, prayed, searched desperately for answers, went with her husband to two Christian counselors who were, in the end, as baffled as she was. Then one day, while working around the house, she prayed "just about every minute of the day, asking God to get through to me on what I needed to do." Next day's sermon was an encouragement to step out in faith if one has a word from the Lord. She wrote,

I remembered your saying on the radio that when people tell you their problems, you often ask them what they think the Lord wants them to do. I was very surprised at the time to find I had an answer to my problem! A simple thing, acting against my feelings. I had tried to do what I thought God wanted me to do then, but decided it was too hard and wouldn't work anyway. I determined to try again. Things did not change overnight, but I persevered. Things changed dramatically. My husband can hardly believe the change in his wife! I can hardly believe it either!

In difficulties of all kinds I've been wonderfully helped by taking time to look at them in the light of Christ Himself. Do you know the hymn, "Beneath the Cross of Jesus"? (If not, you'd find it a great comfort to learn it by heart.) That is where we must take our stand. It was at the cross that Jesus dealt with all our sins, griefs, and sorrows. He calls us to give up all right to ourselves, take up the cross, and follow. This hard place in which you perhaps find yourself, so painful and bewildering, is the very place in which God is giving you opportunity to look only to Him, to travail in prayer, and to learn long-suffering, gentleness, meekness—in short, to learn the depths of love that Christ Himself has poured out on all of us. It is *His* love that must be manifest in you as you quietly submit to what hurts you (Jesus submitted, too); treat your husband as we are commanded to treat enemies—with love (so did Jesus); refrain from taking moral responsibility for your husband (it is not our assignment as wives to do an overhaul job!), except as you daily lift him up to God. This form of suffering is your opportunity to learn to *leave with God what only God can do*. It is His mercy that offers it to you, and don't forget that "Love is His meaning," as Mother Julian of Norwich wrote.

One of the most transfiguring truths I know is that of our being called to *share* the sufferings of Christ. Colossians 1:24 and 1 Peter 4:12-19 put a wholly different perspective on the matter than any of us could have come up with. It's up to God to change hearts. It's up to us to do the simple (not always *easy*), humble, sacrificial thing, and to faithfully leave the rest to God. "Continue to do good" (1 Peter 4:19, NIV), which means just *do the next thing,* whatever that may be (mend those trousers? starch a white shirt?).

> The fretting friction of our daily life,
> Heart-weariness with loving patience borne,
> The meek endurance of the inward strife,
> The painful crown of thorn,
> Prepare the heart for God's own dwelling place,
> Adorn with sacred loveliness His shrine,
> And brighten every inconspicuous grace,
> For God alone to shine.
>
> **Mary E. Atkinson**

Response from a Seminar

"Wish I could say thank you, but I can't. Oh gosh—thank you for *that!* You talked about forgiveness, and my mother, my sister, my neighbor are all sitting there looking at me. All through your talk, they're looking at me. They knew why I needed that talk! My husband is a gambler and am I *bitter!* Bitter, resentful, anxious—all the things you talked about! I'm telling you, God had a funnel from your mouth to my ear. I couldn't believe it. Who told you, I'm saying to myself, who told you about me and my husband? I was taking notes, and I put a box around that word forgiveness. That's for my sister, I said, that's not for me. She's the one that needs that! But it's really for me. God's telling me it's for me. And to think my neighbor gave me the ticket for this seminar for a birthday present. What kind of a friend is that? A *birthday* present! But thanks, Elisabeth."

A Child's Obedience

Questions from a young mother: "How can I train my twenty-month-old to come to me? How many times do I say 'Come here' before I go and grab him?"

The very first time you tell the child to do or not to do something (come here, don't touch, sit still), (1) make sure you have the child's attention; (2) look him straight in the eye (let him know he has *your* attention); (3) speak in an even, normal tone, address him *by name*, give the command; (4) give him a few seconds to let the message sink in; (5) speak his name again, and ask, "What did I say?" Since training should begin long before he is talking, he will not be able to verbalize the answer, but he should obey. Children always are way ahead of their parents' idea of what they can understand. (6) Tell him once more: "Mama said *come*, Andrew." If he does not obey, spank him. After the first time or two of practice, spank after you've spoken *once*.

To make a habit of repeating commands is to train the child to believe you never mean what you say the first time. If the first lesson in obedience is carried out as above, the child learns quickly that you mean exactly what you say. I know it works—my parents taught us this way, and I watched them train my younger sister and brothers. I found that it worked with my daughter Valerie.

If you run after the child and physically force him to do what you say (e.g. grab him when he doesn't come, take something away when he touches it), you are training him not to pay attention to your *words*. He knows he can get away with anything until forcibly restrained.

Now about spanking. The book of Proverbs speaks of the "rod of discipline," (22:15) and says, "Rod and reprimand impart wisdom, but a boy who runs wild brings shame on his mother" (29:15, NEB). "He who spares the rod hates his son, but he who loves him is diligent to discipline him" (13:24, NIV). My mother used a very thin little switch from a bush in the backyard. We knew there was one in every room, readily available to administer a couple of stings to our legs if we disobeyed. Valerie keeps a thin wooden paint stirrer handy in the house, and also in her purse. One or two firm "paddles" on a small outstretched hand are language that an under-two child understands very clearly.

Don't imagine that following this advice will mean that your child will be punished twenty times a day. The wonderful thing about these simple rules is that punishment needs to be used very seldom, *if* you start *soon* enough. If you begin at the beginning to show the child you are serious about obedience, you will not need to undo the months or years of raising your voice, repeating commands again and again, rushing after him. You will have control. The child will be learning to trust the word of authority (which will make it much easier later for him to believe that God means what He says) and your life together will be much more peaceful and happy.

Suppose your child is already twenty months or three years old and you have not taught him to obey? Then you must both pay a price, but I believe it can be done. Set aside a whole morning to start over. Talk to him, tell him how much you love him, tell him, "This morning we are going to learn the most important lesson you will ever have to learn." Let him see that you are in earnest. Start practicing the beginner's rules.

A word of caution: spanking, in my opinion, should be for deliberate disobedience only. When a child spills his milk or stuffs peanuts up his nose or pours your talcum powder all over the carpet, he is not being disobedient. He is only acting his age. You have not forbidden him to stuff peanuts up his nose. If you have, and he does it anyway, spank him. If, in defiance, he dumps his milk on the floor, spank him. But childish mistakes and messes must be

pointed out, and by all means he should be made to rectify them or
clean them up as best he can. Think of punishments that will fit
the "crimes," but reserve the stick or the switch for deliberate disobedience. He will soon learn that when he defies you, a spanking
follows as sure as the dawn follows the night—even if you are in
church or the supermarket. Take him out to the car and spank him.
Explain the whole system to him again (*after* the spanking), if necessary. Put your arms around him, assure him of your love, and
change the subject.

CRCRD

Teaching Children

How many times between the ages of three and ten do children have to answer the only two questions adults can think of to ask them: How old are you? and What are you going to be when you grow up?

The second question may seem innocuous, but is it? In the first place, many children may be distressed at being required to make a choice which is far beyond them. In the second place, it implies that the choice is theirs. This can lead to great confusion later on. The child will grow up physically, but spiritually he will not have begun until he learns that Jesus died not only to save him from sin but in order that he should live not for himself but for Him who died (see 2 Corinthians 5:15 and 1 John 3:16). If a young person has been taught from childhood that he ought to "be something" without at the same time being shown that nothing is better than being God's servant, he may be preoccupied with ambitions and ideals he has gotten solely from the world. If his conception of "where it's at" has nothing to do with the Kingdom of God, he is in for trouble when it comes time to discern the Will of God. He will be setting limits to his obedience, defining the terms of his service. "For My sake" is a concept children can grasp much earlier than we generally suppose. A little boy wrote to me that he was learning to lay down his life for others. To him this meant that sometimes when he would rather play he lay down beside his little sister to help her go to sleep.

Pray that God will show you how to teach your children that life is meant to be lived for God. "You are not the owner of your own body. You have been bought, and at what a price! Therefore bring glory to God in your body" (1 Corinthians 6:20, PHILLIPS). Help your child to understand that the Lord is his Shepherd, and he is a little lamb. The Shepherd will gladly show him the right pathway if he is willing to follow.

Working Mothers

The director of a center for women's concerns said, "Men have always been able to be involved in creative, self-actualizing work." She would like to see more women released from traditional women's work "to be involved in creative work." Creative work, in this lady's view, does not seem to include homemaking and mothering. *Why not!* I would like to ask. And who, for heaven's sake, is going to do the homemaking and mothering? The lady says she felt confused and frustrated when she was doing it, and "struggled with fulfillment." Many women feel as she does. I meet them often. What I long to help them to see is that if homemaking and mothering are the tasks God has assigned to them at present, it will be in the glad offering up to Him of *those tasks* that they will be truly "creative" and find real fulfillment.

There's an eternal spiritual principle here. It ought to be enough reason for anybody. Is there any other reason why I am always telling young mothers to stay home? Yes, two absolutely unarguable ones, and a third interesting one which you can argue about if you want to.

First, the Bible clearly tells *me* (an older woman) to teach younger women "how to work in their homes" (Titus 2:5, JB), or to be "busy at home" (NEB), or be "domestic" (RSV).

Second, children need their mothers. They need quantity time. None of this "quality time" nonsense. Any time which a Christian mother who loves her children gives them should be "quality."

Third, it's very possible that a working mother's income is not nearly so "extra" as may at first appear. Take a look at a study done by Wayne Coleman of Austin, Texas. I think his estimates are very modest. From weekly earnings of $175, subtract:

$17.50...........tithe
35.00...........withholding tax
11.00...........Social Security
20.00...........transportation (.20 mile, 10 miles to job)
7.50...........lunches (these will have to be dieter's specials!)
12.50...........clothes, shoes, dry cleaning
35.00...........child care for one
5.00...........hair and cosmetics
1.00...........office collections, gifts, entertainments
2.00...........coffee breaks, miscellaneous
10.00...........extra for bring-home meals

Net income weekly: $18.50. If you subtract from this the things a woman may buy which she would not have bought if she didn't have "her own income," or that she may feel she deserves because she's working, how much "extra" is there for the necessities that convinced her she needed the job?

Here's a testimony from a young woman in Texas who has no children yet. "The struggle I'm having is even though I work only part-time, there doesn't seem to be time to keep house, be with other women, reach out to the needy and lost. I know the pressures of the world, pushing for 'upward mobility,' figure more into the picture than I realize, making my struggle quite a fight. A part of me wants to quit the job, another part of me isn't that free yet!"

Please—if you're a mother of young children, considering getting a job, will you consider these questions first?

Will your income really be worth it?

Will it increase your husband's tax burden?

Are you giving your best to your family and/or your employer? Former premier of Israel Golda Meir said that a working mother is torn apart—when in the office she's thinking of all she didn't get done at home, and when at home she's thinking of all she didn't get done at the office.

Would your husband be able to do a better job at work if you were doing a better job at home? What are your real motives for wanting to work? Could it be social pressure, boredom, acquisitiveness, pride, and unwillingness to do humble things? Are you trying to prove something?

I know some mothers of young children who in the face of genuine economic necessity have asked God to show them work they can do at home. Then they've gone to the library and read about businesses that can be engaged in at home, or they've been given an "original" idea. It's amazing to hear the answers God has given. "Your heavenly Father knows that you have need of all these things."

Women in the Work World

Because I want to be faithful to what Scripture *does* say I often refer to that passage which tells me, as an older woman, what I am supposed to say to younger women: Titus 2:3-5. But, they want to know, is it wrong for a single mother to work? Is it wrong for a woman who has no children at home to work? Is it wrong for a woman to work because her husband insists on it? The last question is not quite so difficult, since a wife must submit and trust the results to God. I cannot answer the first two. So, for you who so far have found it necessary to work I want to offer some encouragement and comfort.

1. "My God will meet all your needs according to his glorious riches in Christ Jesus" (Philippians 4:19, NIV). Just remember that *God* must be the judge of your needs. Being wise, powerful, and loving, He can be fully trusted to do just what He says.

2. You only know what you have to do *today*. None of us knows the future. Be faithful today—do your work faithfully, thoroughly, honestly, and gratefully. "Whatever you do, work at it with all your heart, as working for the Lord, not for men, since you know that you will receive an inheritance from the Lord as a reward. It is the Lord Christ you are serving" (Colossians 3:23-24, NIV).

3. Be a lady. Betty Greene, pilot during World War II and later with Mission Aviation Fellowship, told me, "I made up my mind if I was to 'make it in a man's world,' I had to be a lady." A true lady is recognized and respected by men. Keep your honor, your distance, and your close touch with God. He will protect you.

4. If you are truly abandoned to the Lord, He will show you if/when He has a different assignment for you. Stay in touch with Him.

CRESCO

Homeschooling

When my daughter Valerie Shepard was homeschooling three of her five children (the other two were preschool age), I asked her what she had discovered about the advantages of homeschooling. Here is her answer:

1. The children have *more time:* to read (aloud and silently); to learn responsibility by doing chores at home; to play (without adult direction) and use the imagination; to listen to and enjoy each other; to learn obedience.

2. Parents need not deprogram or reteach values the child hears for seven hours a day. They have the child's full attention at any time of the day and can give him full attention; he is not absorbing two different value systems daily.

3. Children learn to love each other more. They do not look down on one another in favor of their peers, or in wrong adulation of older children. This society teaches that among children "older is better." That's not right. Having them at home all day allows them to be children without having to "grow up" in the wrong ways.

4. They learn to be servants of one another. The family is a microcosm of the Body of Christ.

After I asked Val to write this I had the fun of trying it out myself. Val and Walt went to South Carolina (taking their nursing baby Colleen) and I had the other four for five (very busy!) days. There was a schedule of chores posted in the kitchen. Daily I reminded them (seldom more than once). The nine-, seven-, and five-year-olds took turns setting and clearing the table, emptying the dishwasher, folding laundry, sweeping the kitchen. Walter (the oldest) and Jim (not quite three) took out trash, the girls cleaned the bathroom. All but Jim made their beds.

School began at nine with Bible reading, singing, prayer, all four joining in. Jim sat on the floor and played while the others studied. Christiana finished her kindergarten work by ten or so, Walter and Elisabeth worked till nearly lunchtime.

Every afternoon there was Quiet Hour. This was a lifesaver for Granny. The three older children were expected to be in their rooms for an hour. They did not need to sleep, but they were to read or find something quiet to do *alone*. (Not once did we have any altercation about Quiet Hour. It had always been a part of their lives, and they *liked* it.) Jim and I lay down together, I read him a Beatrix Potter story, and he fell asleep.

Since we had no car, four of us walked to the grocery store every day, while Walter rode his bike. It was an interesting string of people, Elisabeth hugging (for example) five pounds of flour, Christiana batting things with a box of Saran Wrap, Jim lugging a bag of apples, Granny with a loaded brown bag.

We had poetry readings (Jim memorized with no effort at all) and singing. Everybody learned "Chattanooga Choo-Choo," by mistake, as it were—I meant for them to learn "Praise the Savior" but somehow that one didn't stick so easily, alas! Walter and Elisabeth practiced the piano and played vigorous duets for the rest of us. We made bread and organized drawers and closets and sorted clothes and toys for give-away and picked violets and had a marvelous time.

I should confess this—on the evening of the first day I wasn't sure I'd survive the week. When Val phoned I asked, "How do you do it?" "Mama, I just do what you taught me: don't think about all you have to do, just *do the next thing!*" I needed to be told what I have often told others, and it worked.

Homeschooling is demanding to say the least—but worthwhile. If you are considering trying it, you might want to get Mary Pride's *The Big Book of Home Learning: The Complete Guide to Everything Educational for You and Your Child* (Crossways).

CRECO

Too Many Children?

When I learned that my daughter Valerie was expecting number five, my insides tied themselves in knots.

Val and Walt were both very peaceful about it, willing to receive this child as they had received the others—as a gift from the Lord, remembering His words, "Whoever welcomes this child in my name welcomes me" (Luke 9:48, NIV). But my imagination ran to the future and its seeming impossibilities—"Poor dear Val. She has her hands more than full. What *will* she do with five?" Before she was married Valerie had told me that she hoped the Lord would give her six. I had smiled to myself, thinking she would probably revise that number after the first three or four. Practical considerations rose like thunderclouds in my mind. Money. Another room to be built onto the house. Homeschooling (Valerie was teaching two already). How would the new child receive the attention he needed? *Etc., etc.*

Then I began to look at the advantages. I was one of six children myself, and loved growing up in a big family. Children learn early what it means to help and to share, to take responsibility and to make sacrifices, to give place to others, to cooperate and deny themselves. Why all this turmoil in my soul? Well, because I loved my child! She was tired! Her hands were full! Maybe later, maybe when the others were old enough to help more, maybe... O Lord!

I tried to talk to God about it. Breakfast time came, we ate, washed dishes, school began in the children's schoolroom, and I went to my room, my heart churning. What does one do?

I write this because troubled young women have come to me

not understanding their mothers' reactions to the news of another baby. Was it resentment? Did they not love the grandchildren they had? Why would they not want more? Was it nothing but a meddle-some yen to run their children's lives? Was it a revelation of a worse attitude—an unwillingness to let God be God?

It was this last question that I knew I must wrestle with as I knelt in the bedroom. Most things that trouble us deeply come down to that. I had to bring each of my wrong responses definitely and specifically to God, lay them honestly before Him (He already knew exactly what I was thinking), confess my pride and silliness, and then, just as definitely *accept* His sovereign and loving will for Valerie, for her family, and for me as the granny. Only God knew how many countless others, even in future generations, He had in mind in bringing this particular child into the Shepard family. He was granting this family the privilege of offering sacrifices for Him, participating in His grand designs. YES, LORD. Your will is my conscious choice. Nothing more. Nothing less. Nothing else.

Even though the feelings don't evaporate at once, they have been surrendered, and the Lord knows what to do with them. Mine had to be surrendered over and over again, but He took them,and over the next few days He transformed them. And when the news of Number *Six* was broken to me two years later, I was able to say *Thank You, Lord,* and to add that tiny unknown one to my prayer list.

Evangeline Mary, born November 9, 1988, was lovingly wel-comed by all.

A Child Learns Self-Denial

One of the countless blessings of my life is having a daughter who actually asks for my prayers and my advice (and heeds the latter). She phoned from California one morning, describing the difficulties of home-schooling three children in grades six, four, and one, when you also have a four-year-old who is doing nursery school and a two-year-old, Colleen, who wants to do everything. And since Evangeline Mary was born, a nursing baby now claims attention as well. How to give Colleen proper attention and teach her also to occupy herself quietly for what seemed to her long periods? Valerie was deeply concerned over whether she was doing all she should for that little one.

I reminded her of the women of Bible times—while probably not homeschooling her children, an ordinary village woman would have been working very hard most of the time, carrying heavy water jars, grinding grain, sweeping, planting and cooking while tending children. This was true also of the Indians with whom Val grew up. An Indian mother never interrupted her day's work to sit down with a small child and play or read a story, yet the children were more or less always with her, watching her work, imitating her, learning informally. They had a strong and secure home base, "and so have yours," I told her. "*Don't worry!* You are not doing Colleen an injustice. Quite the contrary. You are giving her wonderful things: a stable home, your presence in that home, a priceless education just in the things she observes."

The demands on Val, as on any mother of small children, are pretty relentless, of course. She does all the housework with the help of the children (a schedule of chores is posted on the refrigerator). People usually gasp when I tell them the number of my grandchildren. "Wow," said one, "it takes a special woman to have that many children." Special? Not really. Millions have done it. But it takes grace, it takes strength, it takes humility, and God stands ready to give all that is needed.

I suggested to Valerie that perhaps she could define the space which Colleen was allowed to play in during school time, and make it very clear to her that school time was quiet time for her brothers and sisters. When Valerie was Colleen's age she had to learn to play quietly alone because I was occupied for a good portion of every day in Bible translation work, or in teaching literacy and Bible classes in our house. She knew she was not to interrupt except for things I defined as "important." At that time there were seldom children of her age to play with, and she had neither siblings nor father, yet she was happy and, I think, well-adjusted. (For a certain period we had the added difficulty of living with a missionary family of six children under nine whose mother felt obliged to be more or less available for her children every minute—they were thought too young to learn not to interrupt. It was not an ordered home, and the mother herself was exhausted most of the time.)

Does this training seem hard on the child, impossible for the mother? I don't think it is. The earlier the parents begin to make the laws of order and beauty and quietness comprehensible to their children, the sooner they will acquire good, strong notions of what is so basic to real godliness: self-denial. A Christian home should be a place of peace, and there can be no peace where there is no self-denial.

Christian parents are seeking to fit their children for their inheritance in Christ. A sense of the presence of God in the home is instilled by the simple way He is spoken of, by prayer not only at meals but in family devotions and perhaps as each child is tucked into bed. The Bible has a prominent place, and it is a greatly blessed child who grows up, as I did, in a hymn-singing family. Sam and Judy Palpant of Spokane have such a home. "Each of our children has his or her own lullaby which I sing before prayer time and the final tucking into bed," Judy wrote. "That lullaby is a special part of our bedtime ritual. Whenever other children spend the night we sing 'Jesus Loves Me' as their lullaby. What a joy it was on the most recent overnighter to have the three Edminster children announce, 'We have *our* own lullabies now!' Matt, who is twelve and who can be so swayed by the world, said, 'Mine is "Jesus Keep Me Near the Cross."'"

The task of parents is to show by love and by the way they live that they belong to another Kingdom and another Master, and thus to turn their children's thoughts toward that Kingdom and that Master. The "raw material" with which they begin is thoroughly selfish. They must gently lay the yoke of respect and consideration for others on those little children, for it is their earnest desire to make of them good and faithful servants and, as Janet Erskine Stuart expressed it, "to give saints to God."

* * *

Surely it was not coincidence that my friend Ann Kiemel Anderson called just as I was finishing the above piece. She had just received little William Brandt, her fourth adopted son. The others were four and three years old and ten months. She was thrilled, and not nearly as exhausted as she expected to be, thankful for the gift of the child and for the gift of the needed grace and strength for one day (and one night) at a time.

"But oh, Elisabeth!" she said in her huskily soft voice, 'when I had only one, I thought I knew all the answers. There is nothing so humbling as having two or three or four children."

I needed that reminder. Jim and I had hoped for at least four children. God gave us one, and that one gave me hardly any reason for serious worry, let alone despair. She was malleable. What "worked" for her may not work for another child, but I offer my suggestions anyway—gleaned not only from experience as the child of my parents and the parent of my child, but from observation of others. My second husband Add Leitch, whose first wife had died, had three daughters. "If I'd only had two, I could've written a book on child training," he once told me. One of them proved to him that he couldn't.

∽∾∽

Serious Play,
Careless Work

When I was a kid we rushed home every afternoon from school, burst into the house to make sure Mother was there where we wanted her to be (she was), and then collected the kids on the block to play Kick the Can or to build playhouses out of wooden greenhouse boxes. Equipment didn't cost us a cent. Adults didn't have to supervise us or drive us anywhere or coach us. We just played. We were kids, and we knew that after-school time was playtime—until it was time to work (practice the piano, set the table, clear the table, do homework).

Something has changed. Educators have gotten terribly serious about play and terribly casual about real physical work. Billions of dollars are lavished on developing crafts which nobody really needs and forms of recreation which people have to be taught to like. We've got "toys to grow on," computer games, play groups, playgrounds. Tiny tots who would have been happy with a few Tupperware containers and some spoons are given fancy mechanical toys that *do* things, and taught that if they make huge messes with finger paints they're being creative, which they didn't know they wanted to be.

I've seen Indian children playing in the river, climbing trees, sliding down mudbanks. But at the same time they were often catching fish or finding wild honey, fruit, or edible snails. They had no toys to play with but they had a marvelous time (at the age of three or four, mind you) building fires, sharpening knives, whacking away at the ever-encroaching weeds. Nobody told them what to do. Child's play naturally turned into useful work. My little three-year-old Valerie was as adept at these activities as the Indians—learned just as they had, by daily observation of adult men and women at work, then by imitation. A girl of ten could weave a perfect hammock; a boy of ten could handle a blowgun and bring home the "bacon," i.e. a bird or monkey for supper. A lot of what they did mattered, and they had much more fun than children who spend a good part of their childhood doing things that don't matter very much to them or anybody else.

Aren't children nowadays often getting far too much of the wrong kind of attention and not nearly enough of the right kind? Does it really make sense for kids of six and seven to be so frantically serious about organized sports and to be geniuses at computer games, but to have no idea how to amuse themselves without a coach, a team, a uniform, an arsenal of weapons, or an expensive and complicated piece of electronic equipment—not to mention daily transportation to and from the athletic field, park, ice rink, anywhere but the back yard? Must they be rounded up, herded, instructed, shouted at, praised, coaxed, and hovered over by adults who are paid money to pay attention to the poor little hooligans in order to keep them out of the adults' hair during "working hours"?

Is anybody paying attention to how a child works? Is it assumed that if asked to rake a lawn he'll do it halfheartedly? Will he sweep the garage in silent fury or will he rejoice in doing a thorough job of it? Will she scrub a sink till it shines and know herself to be a useful member of a household? School teachers desperately try to teach children who have never really labored with their hands to do schoolwork—not a very good place to start, it seems to me. If a child is not given to understand that he has a responsibility to help make the wheels of home run smoothly—if he is not given work which matters, in other words—why should he imagine that it matters very much whether he cooperates with teachers and fellow students? His parents have failed to give attention to a vital matter. Their attention has been elsewhere—on their own interests, jobs, amusements, physical fitness, or only on the child's health and a misguided notion of happiness which leaves out work altogether. If the "quality time" his father spends with him is limited to amusements rather than work, small wonder the child assumes nobody really likes work. His choices in how to spend his time, like his preferences in food, are *taught* at home—by observation of parental attitudes.

The jungle Indian children I knew learned without formal lessons of any kind. They were with their parents more or less all the time—everybody sleeping around a single fire at night, boys hunting or fishing with their fathers by day, girls planting and gathering food with their mothers. It was hard work to survive. They took responsiblity to collect firewood and keep the fire burning. Very rarely did a parent even have to tell a child, let alone nag him, to do his job. It was expected and the kids met the expectations. Nobody over two had much leisure, but they had a lot of fun. I've never seen people laugh so much. It was a peaceful life, a life without anything like the severe stresses and conflicts we have created for ourselves. Wouldn't it be lovely to go back to all that?

But *how are we supposed to do it?* We don't live in the jungle. Children have jungle gyms instead of real trees to climb; plastic swimming pools instead of a clear flowing river; sliding boards instead of mudbanks. The work necessary to keep everybody alive and fed and clothed is done where they can't see it. So far as children can see, it usually has nothing to do with being fed and clothed but only with money. Their parents (often, alas, both of them) tear off somewhere in the morning and come home at night exhausted, having spent their day at who knows what. The newspaper, dinner, and TV take up a chunk of what's left of the day. Football, the child learns by observation, is vastly more important than anything else in the father's life. It takes precedence over everything, rivets his father's attention, something he himself has never managed to do. So he, like his father, seeks escape from home and the responsibilities of home.

Is the situation irremediable? I don't think so. Surely we could eliminate some of the frustration and discontent of "civilized" family life if we took our cues from the "uncivilized" people who work almost all the time (and *enjoy* it) and play very little of the time (without making a complicated chore out of it). Happiness, after all, is a choice. Let your child see that you put heart and soul into the work God has given you to do. Do it for Him—that changes the whole climate of the home. Draw the child into acceptance of responsibility by starting very early. Expect the best. If you expect them to oppose you, to "goof off," to be terrible at two, rude at ten, intractable as teenagers, they won't disappoint you.

It takes longer, of course, to teach a child to do a job than it takes to do it yourself—especially if you have not given him the chance to watch you do it fifty times. It takes sustained attention—the sort of attention a child desperately needs. He can't get too much of that. He needs to be convinced that he is a necessary and very much appreciated member of the family.

What about the sacrifices? We're going to have to make some if we mean to correct our mistakes. Instead of sacrificing everything for money and sports, which most people seem ready to do without a qualm, we may have to sacrifice money and sports for our children. We will certainly have to sacrifice *ourselves.*

But, of course, that is what being a father or a mother means.

෨෧෨

If you could once make up your mind in the fear of God never to undertake more work of any sort than you can carry on calmly, quietly, without hurry or flurry, and the instant you feel yourself growing nervous and like one out of breath, would stop and take breath, you would find this simple common-sense rule doing for you what no prayers or tears could ever accomplish.

Elizabeth Prentiss

෨෧෨

How Much Should Children Work?

"I have four boys, ages sixteen months through nine years. When I ask them to empty the dishwasher the oldest often says it's my job. I feel they need to learn to work and help around the house, but why? I'd like a specific *reason* why he should have to do it. I have nothing against big families, but isn't it possible that older kids have to do a lot of work because Mom keeps having babies and can't handle it all? I often feel guilty. Don't children deserve a childhood?"

Good questions. Let me begin with the last. The idea that a child deserves to play *rather* than work is a mistake. Play is a natural *part* of childhood but so is work! It better be. I think I read that we learn half of all we'll ever know in the first two years! Watch a child who is given a piece of real work that he can do. He is even happier than when at play. When I phoned Valerie one Saturday she was cooking up fifteen meals to put in the freezer. I heard her six-year-old putting carrots through the food processor and he was having a ball.

Now the first question. *Why* should they help? Try something like this: "Because you are a working member of this family, for a start. The only one who isn't is the baby. I'm your mother and one of my most important jobs is to teach you to work. I can cook, you can't, but you can empty the dishwasher, so that's your job. The Bible says if a person won't work he can't eat. I'll cook for you, you clean up for me. Doesn't that make sense?"

Teach children the *joy* of work by your own example. Let them see that you don't hate it. Give *everybody* a real responsibility, starting early. Two-year-olds can empty waste baskets, set the table, pick up toys and put them away, put silverware in the drawer (provide a step stool), hang up their own clothes, help fold diapers, sharpen pencils. Time in teaching is very well spent. I believe that words of encouragement should be the *only* rewards offered for routine work. Giving money or special treats delivers the message that working is beyond the call of duty.

❤️❤️❤️

"...with All Your Mind"

How can parents encourage intellectual pursuits with their children?

A friend who has four boys, the oldest of whom is eight, prints a different hymn and several Scripture verses each week and posts them on a large, stiff cardboard in the breakfast nook. The whole family learns the hymn and verses. She has a chart showing each child's chores. This may not sound very intellectual, but the orderly doing of household chores forms habits of an orderly life, and orderly lives and orderly minds go together. This same mother bought a microphone and small public address system. She has each child stand up at one end of the living room while the others sit in a row like an audience and listen to him recite a verse, a hymn, a poem, or make a short speech. This teaches poise, articulation, the art of speaking up, standing still, keeping the hands relaxed, etc. The same thing could probably be accomplished with a pretend microphone—an ice cream dipper, for example.

Teach your children to memorize! Their ability to quickly pick up anything you repeat often enough is nearly miraculous. One week when I was with my grandchildren for four days, the seven-year-old and the five-year-old learned to repeat the Greek alphabet almost perfectly in that time. I didn't make a federal case out of it, but merely repeated it now and then at odd moments. The five-year-old was quickest to learn it, probably because she thought it was fun while her brother thought it was kind of crazy.

Ask questions at the table which will make children think. For example, God answers prayer—does that mean that God always gives us exactly what we ask for? Help the child to find the answers in Bible stories.

Read aloud to children. My father did this for us as long as we lived at home. He would bring a book to the table and read a paragraph, or share something in the evening as we all sat in the living room reading our own books.

Buy a microscope or a magnifying glass. Study a housefly's leg or the dust from a moth's wing, etc.

Have a globe on which they can find any country they hear named in the news or in conversation.

Teach them to see illustrations of abstract truth in concrete objects. This is how Jesus taught—by the use of parables.

James Boswell, biographer, tells how when Samuel Johnson was still a child in petticoats, his mother put a prayer book into his hands, pointed out the collect for the day, and said, "Sam, you must get this by heart." She went upstairs, leaving him to study it. By the time she had reached the second floor, she heard him following her. "What's the matter?" she said. "I can say it," he replied, and repeated it distinctly, though he could not have read it more than twice.

Was he a genius at that age? Perhaps. But I think it more likely that his intellectual powers owed much to his parents' expectations and patient instruction. Expect little and you'll surely get it.

∽∽∽

Teach Your Child to Choose

Lars and I had breakfast with our friend Barb Tompkins in Tucson. She brought along two-year-old Katy, who behaved very well throughout most of the meal. She interrupted at one point, and pestered her mother, who said quietly, "Katy, you are not in charge here. But would you like to be in charge of Baby Flo?" Baby Flo was a tiny doll she had with her.

I plied Barb with questions about how she rears her children (she has two older boys also). She said she had been helped by Paul Meier's book *Happiness Is a Choice* and had determined to teach her children how to make good choices.

When Katy was about eighteen months old, Barb decided to teach her to stay within the boundaries of their own property, although there was no fence. She set aside a day for this lesson and walked the boundary with the baby, pointing out where she could and could not go, explaining that to step over the line meant a spanking. Barb then sat down in a lawn chair with a book and told Katy she could play. It was not long, of course, before Katy tested the line, then stepped over. In a normal tone of voice Barb called, "Katy, would you come here, please?" That lesson had been learned long before, so Katy came. "Katy, honey, I see you have chosen a spanking," said the mother, and proceeded to give her one. Then she went over the lesson again, explaining why the spanking had been necessary. It was Katy's choice.

It's important, she says, not to label a child *naughty* or *good*, but to point out exactly what he did that was naughty, or what he did that was good. When correction is necessary, Barbara tries always to affirm the child in some way afterwards—"I like the way you picked up your toys this morning."

Barb does not always use spanking for punishment. Sometimes she gives the child "time out," which means she is put into a Port-a-Crib for a little while in order to meditate on her disobedience. If the child climbs out she has "chosen" a spanking. Barb thinks it is very important that the "time out" place not be the child's own bed or bedroom. She doesn't want her children to associate those places with punishment.

During our breakfast together Katy whined for something, and Barb turned to her and said "Katy, you need to make a request." Katy said, "May I please..."

When Katy pulled a pen out of her mother's purse, Barb said, "That is not a choice. But these things are—which would you like to play with?"

Lars and I enjoyed that peaceful breakfast. It was peaceful because Barb was calm, firm, cheerful, and matter-of-fact in her asides to Katy. And Katy was happy, too!

ᏣᏯᏯᏐ

Matthew Henry on
Child Training

When I was the newly widowed mother of a fourteen-month-old daughter, my mother sent me this quotation from Matthew Henry, an eighteenth-century commentator whom my father had been reading aloud to her that morning in April, 1956:

"Proverbs 19:18, 'Chasten thy son while there is hope, and let not thy soul spare for his crying.' Parents are here cautioned against a foolish indulgence of their children, that are untoward and viciously inclined, and that discover such an ill temper of mind as is not likely to be cured but by severity.

"1. Do not say that it is all in good time to correct them, no, as soon as ever there appears a corrupt disposition in them, check it immediately, before it takes root and is hardened into a habit. *Chasten thy son while there is hope*, for perhaps if he be let alone awhile, he will be past hope, and a much greater chastening will not do that which now a less would effect. It is easier plucking up weeds as soon as they spring up, and the bullock that is designed for the yoke should be betimes [before it is too late] accustomed to it....

"2. Do not say that it is a pity to correct them, and, because they cry and beg to be forgiven, you cannot find it in your heart to do it. If the point will be gained without correction, well and good; but it often proves that your forgiving them once, upon a dissembled [pretended] repentance and promise of amendment, does but embolden them to offend again, especially if it be a thing in itself sinful, as lying, swearing, ribaldry, stealing or the like. In such a case put on resolution, *and let not thy soul spare for his crying.* It is better that he should cry under thy rod than under the sword of the magistrate or, which is more fearful, than under divine vengeance."

The language of the eighteenth century sounds a bit stern. We rarely call our children "untoward and viciously inclined," but we see other people's children—in the supermarket, in church, in our own newly decorated living room—who fit that description exactly. Children need a rod, and they need it early. Not a big stick. My parents found that a thin eighteen-inch switch did the trick so long as it was applied at an early age and immediately following the offense. It is important to note Henry's specifying "a thing sinful in itself." Punishment for such things should be different from correction for childish mistakes—spilled milk (have him clean it up if he's old enough), a forgotten chore (have him do that one plus another he doesn't usually have to do).

One grandmother recently told my daughter a method of persuading children to eat what was put before them. When others had finished and a child was dawdling over his plate, she set a timer for five minutes. If the plate was not cleaned it went into the refrigerator to be presented at the beginning of the next meal. "Worked like a charm," she said.

∽∞∾

A Note to Fathers

Are you depriving your son of his sonship? "Hey! Hold it. What?..." Hebrews 12:7 says, "Can anyone be a son who is not disciplined by his father? If you escape the discipline in which all sons share, you must be bastards and no true sons" (NEB). Do you love your son or daughter enough to say no—*and hold to it?* Would you, by cowardliness that fears to make a rule (perhaps because "nobody else" believes in it), treat your child as though you cared no more about him than you would care about a bastard?

But there are some words of caution. "Fathers, don't over-correct your children, or make it difficult for them to obey the commandment. Bring them up with Christian teaching in Christian discipline" (Ephesians 6:4, PHILLIPS).

This reminds me of the way in which the Lord teaches us. He is so patient with us who are so "slow-of-heart." The Shepherd does not make it hard for the sheep to walk in the right paths. He is always trying to make it easier for them, but they balk, they wander off, they don't listen. Children as well as adults are like sheep. They go astray. Fathers are meant to be shepherds. Don't overcorrect. "You fathers must not goad your children to resentment, but give them the instruction, and the correction, which belong to a Christian upbringing" (same verse, NEB). It's balance that is needed. Correct them, teach them. Don't go to extremes. Ask God for wisdom. It's too big a job for any ordinary human being. Look at God as a Father. How does He deal with us? Try to follow His pattern.

CRORD

The Mother of the Lord

We see her first, that little Mary (may I say little? I think she was a teenager), as a simple village girl in a poor home in an out-of-the-way place. She is bending over her work when suddenly the light changes. She raises her eyes. A dazzling stranger stands before her with a puzzling greeting. He calls her "most favored one" and tells her the Lord is with her. She is stunned. I don't believe her thought is of herself (Who am I? or Am I ever lucky!). Mary is troubled. She discerns at once that this has to do with things infinitely larger than herself, far beyond her understanding. What can it mean?

The angel does not weigh in immediately with the stupendous message he has been sent to deliver. He first comforts her. "Don't be afraid, Mary." *Mary.* She is not a stranger to him. He is assuring her that he has the right person. He explains what she has been chosen for—to be the mother of the Son of the Most High, a king whose reign will be forever. She has one question now—not about the Most High, not about an eternal king—those are things too high for her—but motherhood is another matter. She understands motherhood, has been looking forward to it with great happiness. Her question is about that: "How can this be? I am still a virgin." He does not really explain. He simply states a mystery: "The power of the Most High will overshadow you." He goes on to tell her of another miraculous pregnancy, that of her old cousin Elisabeth, well past child-bearing age. "God's promises can never fail," he says. They won't fail for you, Mary. Rest assured.

How will the girl respond? She is at once totally at the disposal of her Lord (she sees that the visitor is from Him). Whatever the mystery, whatever the divine reasons for choosing her, whatever the inconveniences, even disasters (broken engagement? stoning to death—the punishment of a fornicator?) which she may be required to face, her answer is unequivocal and instant: "Here I am. I am the Lord's servant; let it be as you have told me." *Anything, Lord.*

We see her next with Elisabeth, who, by the manner of Mary's greeting and by her own baby's sudden movement in her womb, knows immediately that God has chosen Mary to be the mother of the Lord. They don't sit down over coffee and chatter about the gynecology or the practical logistics or what people are going to say. Mary sings her song of gladness, of thoroughgoing acceptance of the gift, of trust in the Mighty One.

We see her sweating in the cold of the stable, putting her own life on the line, as every mother must do, in order to give life to somebody else. We see her with the tough shepherds, breathlessly telling their story of the glory of the Lord and the singing of the angel choir. Everyone else is astonished (a word which comes from "thunderstruck"), but Mary does not join the excited babble. She is quiet, *treasuring* all these things, pondering them deep in her heart. We see her with the mysterious travelers from the East bringing their lavish gifts. She says nothing as they kneel before the baby she holds in her arms. We see her on the donkey again, on the roundabout journey to Egypt because her husband has been given a secret message in a dream. She does not balk, she does not argue.

We see her in the temple handing over her baby to old Simeon, to whom the Holy Spirit has revealed the child's amazing destiny: a revelation to the heathen, glory to Israel. But to Mary he gives the far deeper message of suffering, for there is no glory that is not bought by suffering: her son will suffer—he will be a sign which men reject; she, his mother, will suffer, will be pierced to the heart. No question or answer from her is recorded. Again we know only her silence.

We see nothing of her for twelve years—days and nights, weeks and months, years and years of caring for the infant, the toddler, the little boy, the adolescent. There is no mention of any of that. Mary has no witness, no limelight, no special recognition of any kind. She is not Mother of the Year. Hers is a life lived in the ordinary necessity of their poverty and their humanity, no one paying attention to her attention to Him. Whatever the level of her comprehension as to the nature of this boy, she knows He was given to her. She remembers how. She treasures all this. She ponders things in the silence of her heart. Did she share any of them with Joseph? Could she? Could he receive them? We know next to nothing of the dynamics between them. She was content to be silent before God.

The apostle Paul tells us we are "hidden with Christ in God" (Colossians 3:3, NIV). There is mystery there, but when I think of the life of Mary, I see some facets of that mystery that I missed when I read the apostle. Hers was a hidden life, a faithful one, a holy one—holy in the context of a humble home in a small village where there was not very much diversion. She knew that the ordinary duties were ordained for her as much as the extraordinary way in which they became her assignment. She struck no poses. She was the mother of a baby, willing to be known simply as his mother for the rest of her life. He was an extraordinary baby, the Eternal Word, but His needs were very ordinary, very daily, to his mother. Did she imagine that she deserved to be the chosen mother? Did she see herself as fully qualified? Surely not. Surely not more than any other woman who finds herself endowed with the awesome gift of a child. It is the most humbling experience of a woman's life, the most revealing of her own helplessness. Yet we know this mother, Mary, the humble virgin from Nazareth, as "Most Highly Exalted."

I am thanking God that unto us a Child was born. I am thanking Him also that there was a pure-hearted woman prepared to receive that Child with all that motherhood would mean of daily trust, daily dependence, daily obedience. I thank Him for her silence. That spirit is not in me at all, not naturally. I want to learn what she had learned so early: the deep guarding in her heart of each event, mulling over its meaning from God, waiting in silence for His word to her.

I want to learn, too, that it is not an extraordinary spirituality that makes one refuse to do ordinary work, but a wish to prove that one is not ordinary—which is a dead giveaway of spiritual conceit. I want to respond in unhesitating obedience as she did: Anything You say, Lord.

> Blessed are the pure in heart,
> for they shall see God.

The Elisabeth Elliot Newsletter (published six times a year) contains articles on contemporary topics such as homeschooling, abortion issues, marriage and sex, widowhood and divorce, and the role of Christians in various social and political arenas. Also included are regular features such as questions and comments by readers, recommended reading and Elisabeth's travel and speaking itinerary. It is supported entirely by donations, but it is sent to any who request it, whether they contribute or not. If you would like to help, a $7.00 donation will cover the cost of mailing the newsletter to you for one year. Those who send more than $7.00 are helping to support others who cannot afford to contribute. Send your name and mailing address to: *The Elisabeth Elliot Newsletter,* P.O. Box 7711, Ann Arbor, MI 48107.